# The Reading Detective Club

# The Reading Detective Club

**Solving the Mysteries of Reading**

*A Teacher's Guide*

DEBRA GOODMAN

HEINEMANN
Portsmouth, NH

**Heinemann**
A division of Reed Elsevier Inc.
361 Hanover Street
Portsmouth, NH 03801–3912
http://www.heinemann.com

*Offices and agents throughout the world*

CIP is on file with the Library of Congress.
ISBN: 0-325-00108-1

Editor: Lois Bridges
Production: Vicki Kasabian
Interior design: Joni Doherty
Cover illustration: Mary Sims
Cover design: Jenny Jensen Greenleaf
Manufacturing: Louise Richardson

Printed in the United States of America on acid-free paper
08 07 06 05 04   VP   6 7 8 9 10

*For Vera Milz, Laura Nebel, and Mary Lou Hess—*
*the first of many wonderful whole language teachers*
*that I've had the opportunity to work with in the last twenty years.*

*For Jacob, Michele, and Scott—*
*and all of the young people who have taught me*
*much of what I know about reading.*

*For Aunt Shirley, my best editor.*
*And for my parents,*
*of course.*

# *Contents*

# *Letter to Colleague*

Dear Colleague:

The Reading Detective Club helps young readers explore the wonders of the reading process and, at the same time, discover their own reading strengths and strategies. I have always been fascinated with the complexities and subtleties of language and literacy. My belief is that literacy learning in school can and should involve the same playfulness and delight as two-year-olds learning their mother tongue.

Frank Smith (1988) talks about inviting our children to join "the literacy club." Kids are eager to join the Literacy Club if they see that literacy is useful and valued by the people they care about. Children must be treated as readers and writers—members of the literate culture. The Reading Detective Club assumes that kids are smart readers and thinkers, and invites them to explore literacy together.

I find that kids love being in a club, and they get really excited about solving their first case. That's partly because I really ham it up. As the "club sponsor" our job is to establish a playful and enjoyable atmosphere for language learning. I wrote these stories initially for my own students. I wanted them to know that language can be fun, interesting, and exciting. I wanted to show them that they are really smart kids who already know a lot about language!

As teachers, I assume you have many ideas about how to use this book with your children. The following pages provide some information, tips, and suggestions. But you know your own children better than I do. Adapt. Have fun.

I hope I have developed a valuable unit of study for you and your students. Enjoy!

Sincerely,

Debi Goodman

# *Preface*

During my first fifteen years as a classroom teacher, reading specialist, and school librarian I have met a lot of kids who have painful misconceptions about reading. There was Jacob, who was repeating third grade. A bright, articulate, and incredibly curious child, he was labeled as a "first-grade" reader. I found he could easily handle materials written with second graders in mind. But Jacob would stop at unknown words and stubbornly refuse to go any further by himself. He was absolutely convinced that guesses or miscues were signs of poor reading.

Michele, unlike her classmate Jacob, was willing to plod along through any text. However, in an effort to sound out and pronounce words, she produced many nonwords and nonsense sentences. She focused so much on "getting the words" that she often lost track of making meaning.

Jacob and Michele made a good pair. Michele would patiently read a text out loud. Jacob, with his experiences and strong oral language background, would supply meaningful guesses as long as Michele was doing the reading. But I couldn't convince these children that they were readers and knew many good strategies for reading.

Jacob and Michele shared a common misconception that *accuracy* is the key to the reading process. Their goal was "getting the words right" rather than comprehending written text. In order to progress as readers, Jacob and Michele would need to abandon their search for accuracy and recognize that *proficient readers are risk takers and that guessing and miscues, or mistakes, are a part of the reading process.*

How could I help Michele search for meaning instead of just "sounding out" words? How could I convince Jacob that it was okay to make guesses in order to make sense of text? How could I push them to work on their own so they would see themselves as capable readers? Like many young readers, both children were fond of the *Nate the Great* books by Marjorie Sharmat. Making guesses and following hunches is the name of the game if you're a detective. Why not place kids in the role of linguistic detectives? And so The Reading Detective Club was born.

**Miscues are often described as "mistakes." However, researchers have found that miscues are an important aspect of the reading process, since they reflect readers' predictions and meaning construction.**

# Acknowledgments

This book is based on my understandings of the reading process, which have developed as I explored the ideas of reading researchers in my own classroom. Kenneth Goodman learned about the reading process from the "miscues" that readers make as they read whole texts aloud. Miscues take place when a reader's oral reading differs from the listener's expectations. Yetta Goodman and Carolyn Burke developed the Reading Miscue Inventory (RMI), adapting the research process for classroom teachers. Their book *Reading Miscue Inventory*, revised and coauthored with Dorothy Watson, helps teachers learn about the reading process as we learn about the readers in our classrooms.

In the book *Reading Strategies: Focus on Comprehension*, Yetta Goodman, Dorothy Watson, and Carolyn Burke provide a wide range of strategy lessons, which help readers focus on meaning construction, the reading process, and meaning-making strategies within the context of a meaningful text. The Reading Detective Club cases are reading strategy lessons, designed to help young readers become more aware of proficient reading strategies.

Carolyn Burke began to explore how readers view reading with her "Reader's Interview of the Reading Process" (Goodman, Watson, Burke 1987). Using this interview procedure helped many of us see that proficient readers often did not recognize their own strengths and strategies. Yetta Goodman, Ann Marek, and others began exploring "Retrospective Miscue Analysis" (RMA), a procedure where the readers, usually those who feel they are not successful at reading, participate in the miscue analysis process. With the RMA procedure, the readers begin to recognize and value their own reading strategies and abilities.

    I "stole" many of the learning experiences in this book. The original "missing word" cases grew out of working with Margaret Lindberg, who used a modified cloze procedure as a silent reading form of miscue analysis. Experimenting with this procedure as a reading teacher helped me see its potential for instruction as well as for evaluation. Ken Goodman has developed learning experiences that help researchers, educators, and preservice teachers see the reading process in action. In particular, the stories "Is Your Mom at Home?" and "The Norful Snig" are based on these exercises (see Goodman 1996, Chapter 4). "The Case of My Own Miscue" is directly borrowed from Dorothy Watson's strategy of "Reader-selected Miscues" (see Goodman and Marek 1996, Chapter 13).

    *The Reading Detective Club* exists because of the encouragement of many teachers who tried the mysteries with their students. I'd especially like to thank Yetta Goodman and Debra Jacobson for "publishing" the trial edition; Katy Kane and Alan Flurkey for editing suggestions; and Lois Bridges for pushing Heinemann to publish this edition. A special thank-you goes to Carol Gilles, who was thinking of pizza when she read "Peoria." As I write, I also remember my aunt, Shirley Rapoport, who gave me some great suggestions on an early manuscript. This writer's text is a transaction built upon transactions with the people I've mentioned above, with teachers I've worked with over the years, and especially with the young reading detectives who have helped me to learn about reading.

# *Introduction*

Over the years I have discovered that many children have negative attitudes about reading, misconceptions about the reading process, or negative views of themselves as readers. If you can't read as well as most of your classmates, being asked to read a book is sometimes a humiliating and even traumatic experience. Timothy was repeating second grade and was still in the first level of the basal reader that his teacher used. It was little wonder that he spent his reading time disturbing other children, running out of the classroom, and getting into fights in the hallway. In my Language and Literacy Center, Timothy would sit for hours listening to stories on tape (purchased from school book clubs), and soon Timothy was reading these wonderful stories to the class.

In recent years educational mandates and outcomes have pushed for higher and higher levels of literacy at younger and younger ages. These mandates often have little regard for developmental growth, experiential background, and individual differences among young children. In many districts first graders and even kindergarten students are already considered "delayed" or even "disabled"—perhaps because they don't know the alphabet or aren't good spellers. Our labels, views, and expectations as teachers and parents are picked up by our students and incorporated into their image of themselves as readers. They are not being invited to join the Literacy Club.

I have also discovered that misconceptions and negative attitudes aren't limited to less proficient readers. You probably know a lot of students like Joe, a very proficient reader who, as a fifth grader, disliked and avoided reading. He stuck with Heathcliff and Garfield for self-selected reading choices. (Yes, I allowed him to read cartoon books. He is the reader, after all.) After months of patience, time for reading, encouragement, and The Reading Detective Club discussions, Joe read a complete novel in March. By the end of March he had selected to read three additional novels.

I recently tried The Reading Detective Club explorations with college students. My undergraduate students have asked their friends (also college students) to read some of the activities. In addition to learning about the reading process, we have discovered that many successful college students, including teacher candidates, get extremely nervous if they are asked to participate in reading tasks or studies. Some report that they are "not a very good reader." These highly proficient adult readers doubt their own abilities and strategies—most likely believing that "accuracy" is the goal of the reading tasks.

Attitude, then, has a great deal to do with being a reader. Children who know that the purpose of reading is to "make sense" of text tend to search for meaning and reject nonsense, looking for texts that suit their own interests, needs, or purposes. They enjoy reading, and so they read a lot. They consider themselves good readers and, as they practice reading skills through reading, they become more and more proficient. They develop a wide range of functional strategies for constructing meaning with a text.

In Reading Miscue studies (Brown, Goodman, Marek 1996), we have found that *all* readers use strategies for constructing meaning. Making sense of the world (or a text) is a driving force in human life. However, if children believe the purpose of reading is "accuracy," they tend to mistrust their meaning-making strategies. Like Jacob, they may rely on adults to provide unknown text. They may become frustrated, unhappy, and resistant when asked to read an unfamiliar text. Or, like Michele, they may attempt to "sound out" unfamiliar texts—producing nonword substitutions. When the readers' goal is "accuracy," their focus is narrowed to letters or words rather than meaning constructions. Their miscues often result in meaning loss.

Proficient readers also produce miscues while reading, but their miscues are more likely to be meaningful substitutions that maintain the meaning of the story. In fact, proficient readers often make highly complex miscues, changing the structure of a sentence or a passage. This is because they are focused on the story meaning and are less concerned with the surface features of the text.

All children have strengths and strategies for constructing meaning. Yet many young readers aren't aware of their own strengths. They may view reading as a school assignment and have little sense of a personal purpose and function for reading. If they are placed in "low" reading groups and receive poor grades, they soon become discouraged and decide that they are poor readers. They begin to actively dislike and resist reading, perhaps even developing behavior problems. They read as little as possible and lose opportunities to grow as proficient readers.

My observations of my students' attitudes and beliefs have led me to conclude that we need to "revalue" reading with our children so they understand the purposes and functions of literacy. We need to "revalue" the reading process so children realize that even proficient readers use cues and strategies to make sense of texts. And we need help our kids "revalue" themselves as readers, realizing their own strength and potential.

During the last three years I have observed a group of children move from kindergarten through second grade in whole language classrooms in inner-city Detroit. Although these children might be considered "at risk," their teachers treat them like readers and writers regardless of their development and ability. The motto "I can" is posted and discussed frequently: I can read; I can write; I can solve problems, and so forth. In interviews, the children identify themselves as "readers." This is because they have all had many successes at "reading" the predictable texts that fill their classroom, such as stories, poetry, charts, nonfiction books, newsletters, signs, daily agendas, and songs.

These young readers have many strategies for constructing meaning with text, even before they have sorted out the relationship between letters and sounds. They can read with a friend. They can read a story the teacher has read to them. They can get help from another student. They can look at the pictures and construct a meaningful text. I was excited to discover (after years of working with discouraged readers like Timothy, Jacob, and Michele) that this group

## *What Does* Revalue *Mean?*

Many of the terms we commonly use to talk about reading are value-laden, often with negative implications. Words like *deficiency, diagnoses and correction, illiterate, reading clinic, remediation, learning disability* and *at risk* tend to imply that less proficient readers are incomplete or disabled and need to be corrected or fixed. Instead, we can *value* children for their language abilities, their smart strategies, and the rich cultural background of knowledge and experiences they bring to the reading process. As we change how we *value* reading and readers, we can help young readers to reconsider their *values* about reading and about their identity as readers. Ken Goodman coined the term *revaluing* to describe this process.

of children strongly view reading as meaning construction. They love books. They are eager and confident with books. They think "miscues" are okay: "After all, I'm just learning." And they almost never produce nonsense words as they read a text. They believe reading means making sense of text.

Our attitudes and beliefs are very important in literacy learning. The Reading Detective Club helps children explore their attitudes and beliefs. However, this book will *not be enough* to change children's attitudes toward reading. I've come to believe that the best change agent is the "can't-put-it-down" reading experience. Once a child has found a book or poem or article that they truly love or need, they are very likely to want more.

Our primary job as teachers and parents is to introduce children to texts and reading experiences that answer their burning questions and speak directly to their hearts. The Reading Detective Club is not a reading program, but it supports and extends a classroom curriculum where students are engaged in meaningful reading and writing experiences for a variety of purposes.

The Reading Detective Club is designed as a series of self-teaching strategy lessons. Working without adult assistance, children learn to trust their own abilities and strategies. After students have solved the mystery, they come together to talk and tease out what they have learned about the reading process. Here's where you are part of the discussion, though the focus is on exploring *what your students have learned* from the "case." The debriefing activities reflect what I have learned from the young detectives in my classroom over the last fifteen years. They are meant to produce thought and discussion and should not be viewed as busywork or as written assignments.

I have tried to write a book to help teachers, parents, and children explore the reading process together. In the section "Readers and Detectives: What's the Connection?" I explain the reading process in more detail. This is followed by a description of how The Reading Detective Club is one component of a language arts curriculum. Next you will find some tips for The Reading Detective Club and an overview of the cases. And finally, I have provided a recommended reading list in case you are interested in further reading.

## Goals of the Reading Detective Club

• **To support a whole language, literature-based classroom.** The Reading Detective Club is not a reading program but part of a strong reading curriculum. The club is meant to support a whole language curriculum, including time for daily reading and writing of self-selected materials and topics; a classroom library with a wide variety of texts; a wide range of authentic literacy experiences; and many opportunities to explore, reflect upon, and discuss a wide range of books and authors. In a whole language classroom, children interact with a variety of texts for a variety of important purposes throughout the day and across the curriculum.

- **To help students *revalue* the reading process.** Reading is a process of constructing meaning with text. Proficient readers read texts that have purpose, relevance, and meaning in their lives. They read *effectively,* using a range of strategies for making meaningful predictions and interpreting text meanings. They read *efficiently,* using the minimum amount of cues from the text in order to construct meaning. Less proficient readers are often confused about the focus and goals of reading. They may focus on "accuracy" as the goal of reading. They may relate good reading to reading quickly. The Reading Detective Club helps students understand that "reading" means making sense of a text, and that "miscues" (or mistakes) are a part of the reading process.

- **To help students *revalue* reading.** Reading is a form of social communication. In the highly literate culture we live in today, reading is essential to our way of life. We read texts daily to find things out, explore ideas, communicate with others, live safely, participate in community events, expand our minds, and so on. Students often view reading as "something you do in school." Without function or purpose, reading is boring and becomes a chore. Kids often discount the proficient reading they do at home. Yet kids are often highly proficient readers of cereal boxes, TV listings, or video game magazines. This club encourages students to explore why they read and rekindle their excitement about reading.

- **To help students *revalue* themselves as readers.** Many students are insecure about their reading ability. They may view themselves as poor readers because they read slowly or make miscues. The cases in The Reading Detective Club help students observe and recognize strategies they are already using. The club helps students become aware that all readers make miscues as they construct meaning with a text. As students solve each case, they begin to see themselves as capable and smart, and they are able to use reading strategies consciously and effectively.

- **To encourage inquiry into language processes.** The Reading Detective Club cases help students discover the reading process for themselves. They are psycholinguists, investigating a process involving both thought and language (reading), and sociolinguists, researching and studying a social and cultural language process (reading). I wrote the cases for students to solve in pairs or teams with little or no assistance from the teacher. As students work in pairs or groups, it's important that they understand that all members of the group have good thoughts and strategies to contribute. The debriefing pages assist the young language researchers (detectives) to analyze and interpret their data. The focus of the debriefings is to allow students to explore and describe what they have learned. Be sure to use the debriefing guidelines with flexibility.

- **To provide a successful and enjoyable experience for all students.** The Reading Detective Club meetings should be fun. This doesn't mean, of course, that using our brains isn't hard work. Students may become frustrated with some of the cases, and should be encouraged to continue to think and guess. If they are able to work out a "hard" case on their own, they will realize just how smart they are! The cases were designed to prove to students that they use language cues and strategies in order to construct meaning from a text. If a case is not a successful experience, talk to the readers about what went wrong and what can be done to turn things around. Feel free to blame my writing rather than their reading. Help the detectives see that they are using good strategies even if they aren't always productive. The whole purpose of this club is to experiment and play around with language. It's important that each "case" be a successful and an enjoyable experience for each reader.

# What Is a Miscue?

Ken Goodman (1996) coined the term "miscue" to describe the times when a child's oral reading differs from our expectations of a reader's response to the printed text. Other terms for miscue—such as "reading error" or "mistake"—have negative implications: that good reading means *accurate* reading and that proficient readers don't make mistakes. Through Reading Miscue Analysis studies (Brown, Goodman, and Marek 1996), we know that *all readers* make miscues when they read. Since reading involves constructing meaning and predicting possible language structures and wordings, we are often thinking ahead of where we are while reading. Miscues are a part of the reading process.

Ken Goodman discovered that miscues provide us with a "window on the reading process." Readers' miscues are cued by the same language systems that cue expected responses. I'm sure you have listened to readers produce an "accurate" oral reading of a text without understanding what they've read. (I have that experience with legal contracts and technical documents outside of my field.) As a result, we can't learn much about readers from "accurate" readings. But the readers' miscues provide a glimpse into their thought processes. Here is an excerpt from Melissa's reading of *Monster Manners* by Joanna Cole:

> *Rose*
> Rosie had just one problem.  ⓤⓒ
>
>                                       *2. meant*
>                     *mother's* | *1. magic*
> She was always forgetting her monster | manners.

Melissa reads: *Rose had just one problem. She was always forgetting her mother's magic . . . meant.* There are three miscues in twelve words (25 percent). If we focus on "accuracy," we might think this text is too difficult for Melissa. But let's examine the quality of miscues first.

When Melissa interprets *Rosie* as *Rose,* she realizes *Rosie* is a character in the story. She uses this substitution throughout the reading without any hesitation or attempt to correct. In reading *Rose* for *Rosie,* Melissa's focus is on meaning, and she is unaware of her miscue. This is a proficient reading strategy, since substituting a familiar name for a less familiar name does not cause any loss in meaning. Later in the text, Melissa abandons this meaningful substitution strategy and spends time repeatedly trying to sound out the name of another character, *Prunella.* Melissa's lack of confidence and consistency in focusing on meaning provides hints that she may not recognize her own meaning-making strengths and strategies.

Melissa starts with a meaningful prediction in the sentence: *She was always forgetting her mother's magic.* Since this passage occurs on the first page of the story, Melissa does not have many semantic (meaning) cues available to predict likely story meanings. While Melissa's reading changes the story meaning, she has used semantic cues to produce a possible and meaningful sentence in this context. A story about monsters might include magic. A young monster might forget something of her mother's.

Melissa is also using syntactic (grammatical) cues. She substitutes a noun for a noun: *magic/manners.* She places a possessive, *mother's,* before a noun, demonstrating her intuitive understanding that possessives are constituents of the noun phrase. Prior to this sentence, Melissa had read the word *monster* without a miscue in another noun phrase: *a perfect little monster.* In this case, she does not expect a word usually used as a noun (*monster*) to appear as an adjective (*monster manners*). Melissa uses her understandings of English syntax as she reads.

Melissa also uses graphophonic cues. Her substitutions look very similar to the expected responses: *Rose/Rosie, mother's/monster, magic/manners.* In fact, most of her miscues (85 percent) are graphically similar to the printed text. These similarities demonstrate Melissa's phonics understandings. When Melissa attempts to correct *magic* to *meant,* her second attempt, *meant,* is more similar graphically to *manners.* However, she abandons her semantic and syntactic strategies. Her meaningful prediction (*She was always forgetting her mother's magic*) becomes a sentence that is neither grammatical nor meaningful (*She was always forgetting her mother's meant*).

From Melissa's miscues, we have begun to describe the profile of a reader. Melissa is able to use a variety of language cues and strategies, but she does not consistently focus on efficient strategies for making sense with text. Melissa appears to view accuracy and phonics strategies as more important than meaning construction. However, this is just the first page. Let's look at another passage that occurs towards the end of the story:

(C)    (UC)
*said Rose*
Something had to be done. And Rosie did it

*dived to the*
*telephone*        (C)        *on*
Without thinking she dialed the phone and said in a nice voice,
(C) *She had a lick on her*
"Hello. We have a leak at the Monster's house. Can you come over please?"

Melissa reads: *Something had to be done, said Rose.* (The circled C above the text indicates self-correction.) [*Corrects*] *And Rosie did it. Without*

*thinking she dived to the telephone and said on* [C] *and said in a nice voice,*
*"Hello." She had a lick on her Monster's house. Can* [C] *We have a leak at*
*the Monster's house. Can you come over please?"*

In this passage, Melissa has ten substitutions and one insertion in
35 words (29 percent). If we just look at accuracy, Melissa did a better
job of reading the first passage. However, it is clear from the quality of
miscues and the self-corrections that Melissa is highly involved in
constructing meaning.

At first glance, some of Melissa's substitutions (*said/and, she/we,*
*had/have, on/in, on/at, her/the*) might cause you to wonder why
Melissa is "missing all the little words." Why does she have miscues on
words she obviously "knows"? In this section Melissa shows us that
when readers are *producing* meanings, they are not simply *reproducing*
the written text.

In the events leading up to this segment of the story, the
monsters' house is flooded. Rosie's mother, father, and her cousin
Prunella have each attempted to call a plumber. But their rude
"monster manners" have caused the plumber to hang up on them. Now
it is Rosie's turn.

Melissa misses the "little word" *And* because she has become
actively involved in constructing a meaningful story. She predicts a
dialogue structure: *"Something had to be done," said Rose.* This is a
meaningful prediction until she sees the disconfirming cues *did it.*
Melissa then self-corrects to *And Rose did it.* While Melissa is aware of
the surface features and is able to self-correct, her focus is on the story
meaning.

Melissa does not correct her substitution of *she dived to the*
*telephone* for *she dialed the phone.* The story picture shows a flooded
room, with the phone floating in the water. Melissa substitutes *dived* for
*dialed.* In order to produce a grammatical sentence she inserts *to,* again
demonstrating her understanding of English syntax. She reads *telephone*
for *phone* because she already knows the meaning of the text and
predicts a meaningful alternate wording. This is one of my all-time
favorite miscues. (Reading Detectives all have collections of favorite
miscues, as you and your students will discover!) Don't you think
Melissa's version is more interesting than Joanna Coles'?

When Melissa substitutes *She had a lick on her monster's house* for
*We have a leak at the Monster's house* she is again exploring the use of
dialogue in stories. This time she predicts narrative rather than a direct
quote. Her prediction involves some complex transformations. She
indicates narrative third person with *she* and *her.* She transforms
present-tense dialogue (*We have*) into past-tense narrative (*She had*).
Again, the meaning of the sentence is the same, except for the
substitution of *lick* for *leak.* When Melissa begins to read the following
sentence, starting with a question marker, *Can,* she apparently decides

that Rose is still talking and corrects the entire sentence: *We have a leak at the Monster's house.*

WHAT WE HAVE LEARNED FROM READERS' MISCUES

- Readers use all of the language systems (semantic, syntactic, and graphophonic) at the same time in order to construct meaning with text.
- All readers make miscues when they read. Miscues are cued by the same language systems as expected responses.
- Miscues provide us with a window into the reading process. We can glimpse the reader's language understandings and reading strategies.
- Proficient readers are actively involved in constructing a meaningful text. They are not focusing on accuracy or surface features of the text.
- The number of miscues does not matter. It is the quality of miscues that are important. Miscues that result in meaningful predictions and interpretations are high-quality miscues.
- Less proficient readers may focus on accuracy and be overly reliant on graphophonic cues and surface features of a text.
- Readers learn to read by reading. It's easier to read an entire story than it is to read a paragraph. As readers read whole and interesting stories they grow more successful at constructing meaning. Use of comprehension-focused strategies increases as readers get more involved and interested in a text.

# Readers and Detectives: What's the Connection?

When I started thinking about readers as "detectives," I began to see many parallels between reading a text and solving a mystery. Ken Goodman has described reading as "a psycholinguistic guessing game." This sounds a lot like detective sleuthing to me.

I start with several important beliefs about reading (and writing):

- **Reading and writing are language processes**. Written texts are not oral language written down. They are language processes with rule systems and structures that are parallel to oral language, but are not the same. Writing is not an "encoding" of oral language into print, nor is reading "decoding" from print to oral language. *When we read and write, we engage with written texts directly to construct meaning.*

- **Reading is a psycholinguistic process.** This simply means that reading involves both language and thinking. In other words, the reader is actively pursuing and constructing meaning. Every reader brings a rich background to the text, including prior experiences and understandings about concepts of the physical world, experiences with written texts, understandings of spoken language, and social and cultural understandings of stories and of human life. *The reader brings meaning to the text in order to make meaning with the text.*

- **Reading is a "guessing game."** We can listen or read very quickly because we are continually making predictions as we read. We predict the next event, the next word, how the text will end, what the author is trying to say, and so forth. As we read, we scan the text and select cues in order to make predictions. We use further cues to confirm or disconfirm our predictions as we continue reading. Predicting and confirming are two major types of strategies we use as we read.

- **Reading involves interpretation.** Readers have different interests, different experiences with the world, different cultural backgrounds, different social communities, different families, and different experiences with oral and written language. In fact, we can probably call reading a socio-psycholinguistic guessing game because language meaning and functions are shaped by our culture and society. Still, *every reader will have a unique interpretation of a given text.*

- **Meaning is *not* in the text.** The *printed text* is a writer's *attempt* to represent his or her own meanings (stories and/or ideas) for readers. But the *printed text* is not the same as the *writer's text*, because the writer uses his or her background and experiences while constructing meaning. The reader brings his or her own background and experiences to the text to construct a meaningful *reader's text*. So the meaning is constructed by a writer or a reader and is not contained within the printed text. The text does contain cues (sometimes called "meaning potential") that the reader uses to construct a meaningful interpretation (or *reader's text*) with the printed text. For this reason, a group of readers will tend to have overlapping or related interpretations of the text. On the other hand, they will often argue over text meanings.

- **Reading involves using written cues *selectively*.** Most of us read silently much more quickly than we can read out loud. This is because we go directly from written symbols to meaning. We *do not* look at each letter and each word. Proficient reading, according to Ken Goodman (1996), is both "effective" and "efficient." "It's *effective* in that the reader is able to make sense; it's *efficient* in that this is accomplished with the least amount of time, effort, and energy. An *efficient* reader uses only enough information from the published text to be *effective.*"

## Reading "Strategies" Are Like Detective "Strategies"

Readers are constantly *predicting*. We make big and small predictions about the next event, the text meaning, the next word or phrase, the point the author is making, or the ending of the story. If our interpretation of the text matches our predictions, we make new predictions and continue reading. If our interpretation doesn't match our prediction, we try a variety of *confirming* strategies—such as self-correcting, rereading, reading ahead, pausing to think, or talking it out—until we come up with a new hypothesis about what "makes sense." Finally, reading involves *integrating* our constructed text into our worldview. We ask ourselves, "So what? What does this text mean to me, my life, my community, and my world?"

Detectives use clues to form hunches or leads. They *predict* possible suspects, motives, and scenarios. They follow these leads until they find evidence that *confirms* or *disconfirms* their predictions. If they find clues that contradict their earlier hunches, they use a variety of strategies, such as rethinking, returning to the scene of the crime, and reviewing all the evidence. As they continue to work with the clues, they construct a "case" that will show "the big picture." They ask themselves, "So what? What does this case mean to the people involved or to our society at large?"

Readers and detectives both use the strategies of *predicting*, *confirming*, and *integrating* in order to successfully make sense of their "case." They also become more proficient, or better detectives, with the experience of each new "case." As we gain experience as readers, we develop a wide variety of strategies, learn which strategies are most useful, and learn how to use our strategies both efficiently and effectively.

## Readers' "Cues" Are Like Detective "Clues"

Proficient readers scan and select a minimum number of cues in the written text, while constantly "guessing" at the story meaning. Readers use a wide variety of cues, including the setting, the title, the format, the letters, the pictures, the wording, the sentence structure, the plot development, the genre, and so forth. We are able to select and make sense of these cues because of our prior experiences, such as knowledge of content and topics of a particular text, experience with the culture and history that produced the text, the oral language background we bring to the text, and our prior experiences with forms and functions of written language.

# *Clues and False Leads: A Set for Ambiguity*

Both readers and detectives must learn what to pay attention to and what to ignore. Detectives must sift out the truth from the available clues. While some clues will help solve the mystery, others may be false leads. Detectives also interpret cues in order to crack the case. Some interpretations may be useful, while others lead the detective off track. Detectives must think flexibly, keeping many possible scenarios and solutions in mind while always digging up the truth. The flexible stance of detectives reminds me of what Ken Goodman calls "a set for ambiguity" among language users.

## *Readers must treat things that are different as if they are the same.*

Reading is fun.  **READING IS FUN.**  *Reading is fun.*
**Reading is fun.**  Reading is fun.  *Reading is fun.*

    In order to makes sense of the above sentences, you have to ignore certain graphic features and attend to others. Do you pay attention to the little feet on the first font? If you look at all of the representations of one letter such as *A,* you'll see that a *grapheme* or letter is not really a tangible object but a concept. *A grapheme is a set of different symbols that we perceive as being the same.* Our eyes *see* the differences, but our brain ignores them in order to *perceive* letters and construct meaning. The same is true of language sounds. Our ears hear differences in sound, pitch, voice, and tone between speakers, but our brain perceives them as the same.

## *Readers must treat things that are the same as if they are different.*

    I *read* the news already. Now I will *read* the sports section.

    Please use this chart to *record* your work because I need a *record* of what you have finished.

The words *read* and *read, record* and *record* look the same. Yet we perceive them differently depending on the context in which they occur. Did you have a problem with the first sentence? You actually can't know how to perceive *read* until you see *already.* Chances are you scanned and selected the cues so quickly that you were unaware of this ambiguity.

    Reading, like detective work, involves a "set for ambiguity." Readers must be flexible—always interpreting and working on hunches, but with an open mind. Because of this flexible stance, we are able to interpret meaning regardless of miscues, typos, or invented spellings. We know what children mean when they write REDEN IZ FN. No computer has the necessary flexibility and set for ambiguity of a five-year-old in constructing and interpreting language.

Detectives scan the territory looking for useful clues that will help them crack the case. They investigate the scene of the crime, interrogate witnesses, and follow a variety of leads. They place these clues side by side in order to develop possible suspects and scenarios. They are able to select and make sense of these clues because of their previous experiences with similar cases, their understanding of patterns of human nature, their background with artifacts (weapons, etc.), and so on.

## Cues and Clues: The Linguistic Systems of Language

Each language system provides "cues" that help us construct meaning as we read. We use all of these systems *simultaneously*. The clues that I discuss in The Reading Detective Club relate to these language cueing systems:

- The semantic system is the system for constructing meaning. Semantic cues are the meaning clues in The Reading Detective Club.
- The syntactic system is the grammatical structure of a text. Syntactic cues are the language clues in The Reading Detective Club.
- The graphophonic system is the rule system for the relationship between letters and sounds. Graphophonic cues are the graphic clues in The Reading Detective Club.

There is also a pragmatic system of cultural and social influences on language. We use this system to know how to speak politely or acceptably in a variety of cultural settings. Since polite speech or writing is often more indirect, we use our pragmatic knowledge to understand, for example, that a question (*Could you PLEASE be quiet*) is actually a directive. Pragmatics comes into play in interpreting humor, sarcasm, and other social and cultural linguistic features. While this is an important linguistic system, I won't describe it in detail. However, our understanding of pragmatics is a part of the social and cultural background we bring to the reading experience.

## Meaning Clues = Semantic Clues

The *semantic system* is the language system we use to construct meaning. In "The Case of the Missing Word," the text reads:

I have one brother and one XXXXXXX.

Note that a hint tells the children that the number of *X* marks has nothing to do with the number of letters in the missing word. The word *brother* cues us about the semantics or meaning of the missing word. We are most likely reading about a mammal/person/family member. The repetition of the word *one* is another cue. It is a member of a matched set with *brother*. The use of a number, *one,* suggests there could be more than one XXXXXXX, so *father* or *mother* are unlikely predictions. While many semantic predictions are possible (*grandpa, dog, headache,* etc.), most readers predict *sister* as the most likely prediction even before reading the additional cues.

Personal and cultural experience influences how we interpret semantic cues. Evan, who has two brothers, initially predicted the missing word was *friend.* When he then read "My XXXXXXX is two," he began to question his prediction. When he read "My XXXXXXX is a real pest," he decided to revise his prediction. While a matched set might include *one brother* and *one friend,* it is unlikely that a *two-year-old pest* would be a *friend.*

Ebony's brothers and sisters are all much older. She has several nieces and nephews her own age. Her initial prediction of *nephew* was abandoned when she saw that the missing word was a "she" named "Lisa." Her revised prediction of *niece* continued to make sense throughout the story. She maintained this interpretation and convinced her detective club team that *niece* was the missing word. (They were right, of course, since *there are no wrong answers.*)

Evan and Ebony's deductions point out the power of whole, authentic texts. *A well-written text provides the reader with cues for self-correction.* Evan and Ebony do not need a teacher to "correct" their initial miscues. If a concept is important, the text provides *redundant cues* that help the reader confirm or disconfirm and refine predictions. In "The Case of the Missing Word," there are *many* semantic cues: matched pairs with brothers, Lisas, females, two-year-olds, and pests. While there are no *wrong* answers, some answers are more informed predictions than others. Evan rejected *friend,* while Ebony's *niece* remained a viable prediction.

Ambiguities exist on the semantic level as well as in the letters and words in a text. The missing word could be *sister* or it could be *niece* or even *cousin. All texts must, by nature, contain ambiguities* because ambiguity is a language property. If authors explained *everything* to readers, texts would be very long and very boring.

The author assumes readers bring knowledge and experiences to a text in order to make predictions, inferences, and interpretations. This explains why some people find auto-mechanics manuals easy to read, while others find them incomprehensible. When authors' assumptions about the readers' background differ from the readers' actual experiences, the result is miscommunication, or what we think of as lack of text clarity.

MAJOR POINTS ABOUT THE SEMANTIC SYSTEM
- Readers use semantic cues as they predict and confirm the meaning of a text.
- Our interpretation of semantic cues depends upon our own background and experiences.

- Authentic texts provide redundant cues, offering opportunities for revision and self-correction.
- Authors assume that readers will predict and infer based on experience and cultural understandings.
- When we use semantic cues we are asking the question: *What makes sense?*

## Language Clues = Syntactic Cues

Studies of language acquisition show that children have learned most of the syntactic (or grammatical) structures and rules of their first language by the time they are three or four years old. School-aged children are able to use the structural rules of their language in order to communicate for a wide variety of purposes. They know how to construct declaratives, imperatives, negative statements, and questions. They know the function and placement of nouns, verbs, prepositions, determiners, adjectives, adverbs, conjunctions, and more. In short, they have an amazing amount of *linguistic understandings*.

This does not mean our students are able to *define* or *discuss* these structures and rules. While they have the *linguistic understandings* needed to *use* language, they may not have the *metalinguistic understandings* needed to *describe* language. We need to separate these two types of linguistic understandings and abilities in order to understand how we use the syntactic structures of language when we read.

All of us (kids included) make good use of syntactic cues when we are reading. Melissa's miscues (page 8) show her use of syntactic strategies. When she substitutes *dived to the telephone* for *dialed the phone*, she inserts *to* in order to construct a syntactically acceptable verb phrase: *she dived to the telephone*. This miscue shows that readers are involved in language construction and that reading is not a simple matter of word recognition.

In the Reading Detective Club, I use nonsense stories to help young detectives become aware of their intuitive sense of English syntax and how they use it when they read. At the same time, the club members learn that we can use syntax to manipulate written language *without understanding the text meaning*. Consider the following "sentence":

The mampy gruffle parstinked the bixton sirky snupples piskfully.

Now answer these questions:
1. What did the mampy gruffle do?
2. Who parstinked the sirky snupples?
3. How did the gruffle parstink the sirky snupples?
4. How many sirky snupples were there?

I can continue to construct nonsense questions and you can continue to answer them because you intuitively know how noun phrases and verb phrases are combined to ask and answer questions.

You recognize the use of adjectives and adverbs without knowing what they mean.

For example, using that sentence as a reference, are the following sentences syntactically acceptable? (It helps to say them out loud.)

5. The mampy gruffle piskfully parstinked the bixton sirky snupples.
6. Piskfully the mampy gruffle parstinked the bixton sirky snupples.
7. Gruffle mampy bixton parstinked the the snupples piskfully sirky.
8. The gruffle mampy parstinked the bixton sirky snupples piskfully.

If you decided that #5 and #6 are grammatical, you were right. But did you know that #5 and #6 are grammatical because of an adverb transformation rule that states that the adverb, while part of the verb phrase, can be moved to other locations in the sentence, such as before the verb (#5) or before the noun phrase (#6)? It doesn't matter if you can *state* this rule or not since you have enough "linguistic knowledge" to *know* this rule intuitively.

If you guessed that sentence #7 is *not* syntactically acceptable, you were right. We all have a strong sense or intuition of what "sounds right" when we're speaking, listening, reading, or writing in our first language. Sentence #7 does not have the recognizable noun phrase and verb phrase structures that we use in English.

What about #8? The change here was more subtle. Did you guess the sentence is not acceptable? In English, the adjective *mampy* must precede the noun *gruffle*. This "problem" might not be picked up by a speaker of Spanish or French, where adjectives are expected to follow the noun in the noun phrase.

When I talk about syntactic rules, I'm not talking "proper English"—those "rules" are confusing because they often conflict with *common usage*. I'm talking about our intuitive understandings of the rules and structures of the language that we speak (and read). A linguistic explanation for why these structures do or don't "sound right" can be complicated, and even a subject of extensive study. But, as language users, we all use the syntactic system on an intuitive level in order to "read" the previous sentences and determine whether or not they are grammatical.

The sentence "The mampy gruffle parstinked the bixton sirky snupples piskfully" demonstrates that *syntax* and *semantics* are different systems. We can construct sentences that are syntactically acceptable but not meaningful. However, we can't construct a sentence that is semantically acceptable (meaningful) without also being syntactically acceptable (grammatical). In order to construct meaningful language, we must use syntax and semantics *together*. In the sentence "I have one brother and one XXXXXXX," the syntactic pattern (*one XXXXXXX and one XXXXXXX*) provides an important cue (matched pair) that helps us use the semantic cue (*brother*).

We don't have to teach kids the rules and patterns of English

## *What if English Is a Second Language?*

I have been talking about the intuitive semantic and syntactic understandings of first-language speakers, but what if English is a second language?

First, I support bilingual or first-language programs that provide an opportunity for children to learn to read in their first language. *Providing opportunities for children to become readers in their home language allows young readers to bring a rich set of linguistic understandings to the reading process.* When children are literate in their first language, they bring written language strategies and understandings to literacy learning in a second language. Even a monolingual English teacher can provide these opportunities. For example, I once visited a classroom in San Francisco where a group of Cambodian children were involved in literature study of a Cambodian folktale with the help of paraprofessional.

Readers who read English as a second language may have *different* intuitive understandings about language structures than readers whose first language is English. It's important to remember that children who read English as a second language actually have *more linguistic resources* to bring to the reading experience. Second-language readers, bringing linguistic understandings from two or more languages, may need more time to scan and select appropriate cues and organize them into meanings, but this doesn't mean they are less able to construct meaning with text.

When reading orally, second-language reading detectives may predict structures that are syntactically unacceptable. These syntactic structures may relate to rule systems from the first language. Or, they may relate to unfamiliar or confusing structures in the second language. It *is* possible for a second-language reader to construct meaningful language without producing syntactically acceptable structures. We can help second-language reading detectives by focusing on reading and writing as meaning construction and allowing them to learn language structures through experience. In addition, we can learn about the structures of their first languages in order to help them share their linguistic knowledge with the class.

grammar before they become readers and writers. (In fact, these rules are so complex we are probably teaching them nonsense when we try.) Like us, young readers are already making use of syntactic cues intuitively as they read. The Reading Detective Club helps kids understand that we use syntactic cues when we are reading. The Reading Detective Club cases will prompt club members to begin to discuss and describe the syntactic cues they use intuitively. In this context, we can introduce linguistic terms like "nouns," "verbs," and "adverbs" because they are useful in the discussion and make a lot of sense.

MAJOR POINTS ABOUT THE SYNTACTIC SYSTEM
- School-aged children already know most of the syntactic structures and rules of their first language. We don't need to teach them these rules.
- We use our understandings of syntactic structures and rules intuitively when we use oral or written language.
- Being able to use language (linguistic understandings) and being able to discuss and define language (metalinguistic understandings) are two different kinds of understandings.
- Using syntactic cues without semantic cues will produce nonsense. We can use the syntactic structure to answer "comprehension" questions without understanding the text.
- We must use the semantic system and the syntactic system at the same time in order to construct meaning.
- When we use syntactic cues we're asking the question: *Does this sound like language?*

## Graphic Clues = Graphophonic Cues

*Phonology*, or the sound system, is the *signal* level of oral language. *Phonemes* (sets of language sounds) are *symbols* that *signal* us to start *perceiving* meaningful language. *Phonemes* don't have meanings. We assign meanings to them when we combine them to construct words, sentences, conversations, and stories. When we hear language sounds, we first *perceive* them as language and immediately begin to predict and construct meanings. Our comprehension depends on our *perceptions*. A monolingual English speaker listening to Greek phonemes, for example, will hear phonemes that "sound Greek" but will not *perceive* meanings—thus the expression "It's all Greek to me."

*Graphemes* (forms of letters) are the *symbols* we use to construct written text. When we look at grapheme strings (text), we *perceive* language and begin to predict and assign meaning, function, and structure to the text. We also *perceive* graphemes when we look at a letter, because a *grapheme* is not one symbol but a set of symbols. We *perceive* the following symbols as the same grapheme although they are very different in appearance.

**A**, a, A, *a*, 𝒜, *a*, 𝔸, **a**, a, **A**

We *perceive* combinations of graphic signals as words, sentences, and written discourse (stories, letters, newspapers). A monoliterate English reader scanning Chinese characters may perceive them as language, but will be unable to construct meaning with them.

Readers scan and select written symbols in order to construct a meaningful text. We do not "translate" written symbols into sounds when we read, but we perceive language and begin sampling and selecting graphic cues while at the same time constructing meaning. *We must bring our experiences and meanings to a text in order to perceive written symbols as meaningful. There is no meaning in the language symbols.*

In alphabetic languages there are relationships between the oral and written symbol systems, described in the study of reading as "the graphophonic system." In The Reading Detective Club, the graphophonic cues are called "graphic clues."

When thinking about the reading process, it's important to consider that not all written languages are organized alphabetically, with a relationship between letters and sounds. In nonalphabetic systems, such as Chinese, written characters directly represent concepts rather than sounds. There are advantages to both written systems. Alphabetic languages use fewer symbols because there are a finite number of language sounds while there are an infinite number of concepts. Chinese characters, on the other hand, have the advantage that the same graphic symbols can be read and comprehended by speakers of a variety of oral languages and dialects (Cantonese, Mandarin, and Taiwanese, to name a few).

There are also some nonalphabetic systems in alphabetic languages. The symbols *1* or *8* relate to concepts rather than sounds. You were probably taught that the numeral *8* is the *symbol,* while the related number is an abstract concept. In other words, we see numerals and we perceive them as numbers. How do you pronounce these

I could not think of a good, common-usage substitute for *graphophonic clues* to be parallel with *meaning clues* and *language clues.* So, I use the term *graphic clues* instead of *letter clues,* because graphic clues may include punctuation, spacing, formatting, and design. Unfortunately, while *meaning clues* and *language clues* describe language systems in both oral and written language, *graphic clues* only refers to written language. For this reason, some teachers may prefer using the more accurate term *graphophonic clues* with their students.

symbols? Does *1* stand for *eins, one, uno, udin,* or something else? These numerals are useful around the globe because they represent related concepts regardless of the sounds of the language. Numerals are also efficient because we can write long spoken strings such as "one million, five hundred and fifty-nine thousand, three hundred and sixty-two" much more quickly as *1,559,362.*

Like all graphemes, the meaning we assign to numerals depends on their context. The numerals *1* and *8* have different meanings in these combinations: 18, 81, 18%, 1/8, $18. The meanings differ again if we place them in a larger context, such as 18 pennies, 18 minutes, 18 lbs, January 18, or 18 classrooms. Graphic cues can not be interpreted unless we see them in a full, meaningful context. *The syntactic and semantic systems must be available to the reader in order to construct meaning with graphophonic cues.*

I bring up nonalphabetic written language because we sometimes think of reading as a process of decoding letters into oral sounds. Instead, in each written system we scan and select graphic cues while at the same time we use syntactic and semantic cues to construct meaning. The reading process works the same way in every written language system whether alphabetic or nonalphabetic. Readers sample and select cues in order to construct meaning.

## So What's Phonics?

In alphabetic languages readers construct rules about the set of relationships between letters and sounds. These "phonics rules" are very complex and often inconsistent for a variety of reasons:

- *Historically, oral language changes at a more rapid pace than written language changes.* For example, the words *night, sight,* and *fright* come from English's Germanic roots. The letters *gh* represent a throaty sound such as the German *nacht.* While the sound was dropped from most English dialects, the spelling pattern remains.

- *English has borrowed many words from other languages.* At the time of the Norman Conquest, English imported a very large number of words from French: for example, *garage, beautiful, ballet,* and *unique.* We have also borrowed from Spanish (*patio, rodeo, Los Angeles*), Yiddish (*kosher, chutzpah*), and many other languages. Because these languages have different spelling systems, English phonics rules involve many different spelling patterns for the same phoneme or sound. For example, the phoneme /š/, commonly spelled *sh* (*shut*), can also be spelled with *ch* (*Cheryl*), *s* (*sugar*), *ti* (*notion*), or *ss* (*Russian*).

- *The morphemic system, or system of wordings, influences how words are written.* When you say the words *boys, desks, trumpets, tables* out loud, you will hear different final *phonemes:* /s/ or /z/. However they are all spelled with the same *grapheme: s.* The letter *s* in these words represents the *plural morpheme* rather than the pronunciation. Root meanings of a derivational word also influence spelling. The word *soften* includes a silent *t* because of the spelling of *soft*.

- *Language variations and dialect difference also influence the graphophonic system.* For example, the grapheme *e* in *pen* might be spoken with the phoneme in *bin* (/pɪn/) for some readers, while other readers will use the phoneme in *bed* (/pɛn/). Both readers understand that they are reading about something you write with, so there is no "reading problem." But "phonics" rules vary depending on the spoken language or dialect of each reader.

- *Written language rules are conventional across oral language variations and dialects.* How do you pronounce *almond? apricot? crayon?* My version of *crayon,* which rhymes with *man,* was incomprehensible to teachers in Alabama who have two syllables, *cray- on.* You might say something in between. *The written form is conventional, but the phonics rules vary depending on the oral language of the reader.*

The complexity and ambiguity of graphophonic rules can be very confusing to writers. Most of us continue to make spelling miscues as adults. However, these miscues do not prevent us from constructing a comprehensible written message. Young writers can also successfully negotiate our confusing graphophonic-phonic system by using "invented spellings." When children are encouraged to write freely with a focus on constructing a message, they gradually construct the graphophonic rules and social conventions of written language. Invented spellings are based on children's current set of understandings about the letter patterns they relate to the sounds in their own oral language. *As we use reading and writing to construct meaning, we learn the complex graphophonic structures, patterns, and rules in the same intuitive way that we learn the syntactic structure.*

The variations in English spelling patterns I've just described are actually *not* a big problem for beginning readers because we *do not* rely exclusively on letter-sound relationships when we read. As readers, we use the other language systems to help us assign meaning and structure to words and letters. Readers' perceptions, predictions, and interpretations of the graphic symbols are also supported by the type of text we are reading, our experiences with that type of text, our experiences with oral stories, our listening experiences with texts, our understanding of the topic, the contexts (such as time and place), and our purpose for reading.

It would be inefficient to look at every letter, or even every word, when we read. ("The Case of the Missing Mom," on page 95, certainly proves that we don't. Can you find all ten mistakes?) Instead, we sample the graphic cues available as we construct meaning with a text. Graphic cues are important, since we perceive texts visually with our eyes. But our mind quickly takes over, organizing the symbols into meaningful language.

TO SUM UP

- The graphophonic system is the symbolic language system.
- When we look at graphemes, we *perceive* meaningful language.
- In all written languages, readers use graphic symbols selectively to predict and construct meanings.
- In alphabetic languages, there is a set of relationships between letters and sounds. This set of relationships is commonly called "phonics."
- Phonics rules are complex and ambiguous. Many spoken English forms have changed historically, while written forms have remained the same. In addition, English has borrowed the written forms of many other languages. Graphophonic rules are also influenced by *morphemes* or word meanings.
- Phonics rules (the set of relationships between sounds and letters) will vary depending on the spoken language variation or dialect of the reader.
- The graphophonic, syntactic, and semantic systems must be used *at the same time* in order to construct a meaningful text.

Young writers and readers will learn the graphophonic structures, patterns, and rules if they are able to explore them while focusing on writing and reading meaningful texts.

**Are All Cues Created Equal?**

Are all three language systems equally important in constructing meaning? Consider this sentence:

Please grick your zines before luffing.

Your graphophonic strategies allow you to "accurately" pronounce the unfamiliar segments. You might associate these "words" with others and guess that *grick* rhymes with *brick*. You might use knowledge of spelling patterns, guessing that the *e* in *zines* is silent and the *i* is stressed as in *vine*. You might assume that the double *ff* in *luffing* suggests the *u* sound is pronounced like *bluff* instead of *compute*.

Your syntactic strategies allow you to guess at the function of these "words." You know that *luffing* is a progressive verb (even if you didn't remember the term "progressive verb"). *Grick* appears to be a verb, and *zines* is most likely a plural noun, something that is tangible. (Well, maybe not—are you thinking of possible meanings?)

## *Where Does Phonics Instruction Come into It?*

Phonics is one of the language systems we use when we read. However, "phonics instruction" often introduces letters and sounds isolated from the meaning, function, and social context of authentic texts. Historically, many teachers and researchers assumed that small bits of information, such as letters, are easier to handle than big bits of information, such as stories. Most reading educators now believe that the graphophonic system is symbolic, highly complex, and difficult to analyze and understand. Language includes meaning, syntax, and symbols. Therefore, the smallest "bit" of language children should be offered is a whole text within a functional setting with the full richness that written language offers.

Phonics instruction focuses the reader's attention on accurately pronouncing words rather than constructing meaning. This can make reading very frustrating and very difficult. It's hard to construct meaning if you're only looking at the letter cues in one word. This history of phonics instruction has lead to a popular, all-purpose reading strategy called "*sound it out*." This strategy is so widespread that children who are taught to focus on meaning will often say "I sounded it out" if they are asked what reading strategy they used.

I have even had students tell me they "sound it out" in the detective cases with missing words and no graphic cues. "Sound it out" is just one among many possible reading strategies—and not a particularly effective one at that. The Reading Detective Club provides children with a more complete view of the reading process. They are introduced to three language systems. They identify and explore a wide range of strategies that readers use in order to make sense of what they are reading.

So we can use graphophonic strategies and syntactic strategies without constructing meaning. *But is this reading, if we aren't comprehending?* A focus on *accuracy* does not help children construct meaning with a text. It is really a mistaken goal, since all of us interpret text differently.

I think we would all agree that the goal of reading is comprehension.

The semantic system is at the heart of the reading process. A reader should first ask "Does this make sense?" or "What would make sense?" before focusing on letters or words. At the heart of reading is meaning.

## *Why Study Language in the Elementary Grades?*

I believe we learn language through using language to interact with others and to learn. For this reason, I have debated whether it is appropriate to focus on language processes or systems with elementary-age students. I have seen how readers lose track of "making sense" when they focus on sound-letter relationships and how writers get distracted from their message and craft if they are focused on correct spelling, grammar, and punctuation. I also feel that time spent focusing on language forms could be spent speaking, listening, reading, and writing.

If you're like me, you've had plenty of negative and boring experiences with language study in primary or secondary school: usually the memorization of phonics, grammar, and spelling rules. If you've taken a linguistics class, you know that language systems are complex and difficult for many adults to describe or understand. When we break language down to its component parts, they become abstractions that are difficult to learn about. That's why it's easier for kids to read whole books and stories rather than letters and words.

In addition, we don't have to understand or explain the rules of language systems *explicitly* in order to use language. As language users we know these rules and processes *implicitly*. Learning to listen, talk, read, and write involves constructing these rules as we interact with others in authentic social contexts. When we focus on the ideas we're trying to communicate, the structures fall into place. For this reason we try to teach language within contexts where we are communicating rather than as a subject in itself.

So why focus on the study of language at all? As I've stated before, students do hold many strong beliefs and attitudes about language, partly as a result of bad experiences with language study. These beliefs and attitudes affect how kids approach reading and writing and how they feel about themselves as readers and writers. Based on their beliefs about reading and writing, children decide to join the literacy club or to opt out. (Based on the beliefs of the people around them, they may be invited to join or be left out.)

There are children who feel sick when they see a book and who go to great extremes to avoid reading. How do we help children to see language as interesting, to approach it without negative evaluations, to see themselves as having linguistic strengths?

## Studying Language Like Linguists

The best way to learn about writing is to be a writer. The best way to learn science is to act like a scientist. When I thought about how kids might learn *about* language, I turned to the people who got me excited about and interested in language as a field of study: linguists, sociolinguists, psycholinguists, and anthropologists. However, I didn't want to teach kids a list of rules that linguists have discovered about how reading works. *Instead I want kids to know how the people that study language investigate language.*

Sociolinguists look at language within whole conversations, books, families, and cultures and ask themselves "How does language work here?" "What purpose does language serve?" "Who can say what and to whom?" and even "What rules do language users use?" Rather than teaching kids language rules, *I want kids to become linguists,* to consider how and why people like to investigate language. For linguists, language "rules" are structures we can explore and discover, and not prescriptions that we are all required to follow.

The Reading Detective Club is a process of studying language through inquiry as linguists study language. The investigations are "rigged" so kids will discover some ideas and theories that challenge some of the negative views and misconceptions they may hold as young readers. However, the language study takes place through whole stories (the cases) to assure that kids have all of their language resources available to them. In addition, the club format provides the support of the social, collaborative aspects of language learning and research.

The Reading Detective Club is based on beliefs and assumptions about language and language learning that I have learned through language study:

• **Reading and writing are language, and all language is rule-governed.** In order to use language, we implicitly understand language rules. This is true of all languages and dialects, and all language users. Language use is never random. Even the mistakes we make as speakers and writers or listeners and readers are understandable if we understand how language works.

• **Language is social and personal.** Language is used to communicate feelings, thoughts, and ideas. Even more important, language is used to establish and maintain social connections and cultural memberships. Language learning involves social membership. We learn to speak the language of the people who care for us and the people we care about. We learn to speak the language of the community and culture that we live in. In order to learn language or literacy we must see ourselves as a member of the group that uses that language. As teachers, we must be aware that language and language learning are closely associated with a child's social, cultural, and personal identity.

## Dialect and Reading

Tony, an African American second grader, is reading *The Three Billy Goats Gruff*. When the first billy goat crosses the bridge, Tony reads: *"'Who's that tripping over my bridge,' roared the Troll."* When the last billy goat crosses the bridge, Tony reads the same printed text: *"'WHO dat trip-trapin' ova' my bridge?' roared the Troll."*

Tony's reading of the text demonstrates several points about dialect and reading. In reading *The Three Billy Goats Gruff*, Tony *code-switches* from a language variation expected at school to a variation he speaks in his home community. Tony's use of his home language (African American Vernacular English) occurs when he is very involved and caught up in the story. Reading in his home dialect *demonstrates Tony's comprehension* and increased involvement in the text.

This example also shows Tony's awareness, as a second grader, of the English variation expected by his teacher in school. He is able to produce a version of the text similar to spoken dialect of his European American teacher. As a young child, Tony has a rich resource of spoken language variations to draw from as he reads.

Since dialect differences are often a concern to reading teachers, I think it's important to make a few points about dialect and reading.

• **We all speak a dialect of English,** and we all read in our own dialect. However, unless we speak a low-status variation of English, we don't notice the language features that *mark* our own dialect. (How do you pronounce *and* in *bread and butter?*) Teachers are much more likely to notice the dialect features of students in their classrooms who come from regions or cultures that differ from their own.

• **All cultural and regional language variations are "good" language.** Every variation of English is entirely capable of meeting the communication needs of speakers. Some dialects may be less prestigious, generally reflecting the political and economic status of the speakers. However, all dialects are equally complex and expressive. We should avoid value-laden terms such as "good" or "poor," "proper" or "improper" English. Instead, we can talk about and explore how dialect "variations" are based on where we live or our cultural membership. Some linguists use the term "language of wider communication" rather than Standard English to describe the language we use to communicate across and between English language dialects.

• **Children who speak a low-status dialect of English (or a second language) have dual language resources to draw on.** It is important that we see a dual language or dialect background as a resource rather than a deficit. Children who speak a low-status dialect have a dual language background and bring the resources of their home dialect to speaking and reading in school. Children who speak a low-status dialect tend to be very sensitive to the language of the teacher or school community. We must respect and celebrate the language children bring to school so they also see their home language as a resource for language learning in school.

- **When readers use their own language to construct meaning, they are demonstrating comprehension.** We all interpret text using our own language. When readers produce miscues that reflect their own language or dialect, they are usually showing their involvement and comprehension of the text. When we ask if a reader is constructing meaning, we need to ask "Does this sentence make sense in the dialect of this reader?" This means that teachers must become knowledgeable about the language of their students.

- **Correcting a reader's dialect variations is confusing and counterproductive. When readers use a dialect variation, they are demonstrating their understanding of the text.** If their language is corrected, readers become comfused as their attention is focused away from "making sense" and toward "correctness." As I've shown previously, a focus on accuracy actually makes reading more difficult.

### Suggestions for Exploring Language Variations

- If children's responses to cases involve dialect features, it is an ideal time to talk about language variations. Children are already looking at how their own "solutions" to the cases differ from their friends', and thinking about how different backgrounds and experiences influence reading. It is easy to explore how different language and cultural backgrounds may produce different responses.

- Be sure your classroom library includes many of the writers who make use of home dialect when they write. (Patricia McKissack, Eloise Greenfield, Mildred Taylor, Walter Dean Myers are a few examples.) Introduce some of these books to the class and encourage children to talk about language as they discuss the texts. This is a good opportunity to stress the beauty and expressive capabilities of all language variations.

- A great resource for language study is the printed lyrics of rap songs. Rap musicians have invented their own spelling system for representing dialect variations. (You'll want to preview lyrics first.)

- Be careful not to *mark* certain variations, such as African American language, by looking at how they "differ." Children may begin to think of European American variations (and culture) as "normal." Children can be encouraged to look for "interesting language" in a wide range of texts.

# Supporting the Principles
# of a Whole Language Curriculum

The Reading Detective Club is not a language arts program, but one small component of a comprehensive language arts curriculum. The following chart shows how "language discussions" are a small part of a language arts curriculum that builds on authentic learning experiences where students use language to learn.

## Authentic Reading and Writing Experiences
### 50 to 70% of Total Instructional Time

- Reading self-selected books, magazines, newspapers, or comic books, independently
- Writing on self-selected topics and genres
- Reading a book with a partner
- Writing with a partner or group
- Listening to a story on a tape or video player and reading along
- Listening to a story read—or told—by a teacher, student, parent, or visitor
- Reading a book out loud to a teacher, younger student, classmate, parent, principal
- Participating in a shared reading and writing experiences based upon class discussions, books read
- Participating in choral reading, songbooks, reader's theatre, dramas, and plays
- Taking part in literacy experiences in learning centers, such as using a notepad next to the phone in the playhouse
- Experiencing literacy across the curriculum
- Communicating with parents and school community: newsletters, agendas, programs, tickets
- Reading nonfiction books for inquiry, interest, and investigations
- Writing "field notes" based on observations of nature, science experiments, class pets
- Taking notes while reading or listening
- Writing reports or informational texts
- Reading and writing charts and signs to organize classroom life
- Reading and writing charts, diagrams, and graphs to organize learning experiences
- Reading or writing personal communications such as letters, notes, e-mail
- Writing to express self, such as writer's notebook, dialogue journals, diaries

## Reflection and Discussion of Texts
### 20 to 30% of Instructional Time

- Literature discussion groups—a small group discussing a book together
- Writer's groups—small groups for writers to share their work and get feedback for revision
- Author's circle discussions—class meeting for sharing finished works or works in progress
- Read-aloud discussions—discussions of students reactions to stories read aloud
- Reading conferences—teacher meets with reader to read together, talk about reading progress
- Writing conferences—teacher meets with writer to discuss progress, assist with revision

- Reading partners—students talk with a classmate about the texts each student is reading
- Dramatizations—responding to texts in plays, skits, choral readings, reader's theatre
- Reading response journals—students reflect on books read independently
- Self-evaluation—students reflect on own reading and writing
- Peer responses—peers provide reflective responses to writing or reading of classmates
- Fine arts—students represent text interpretations through art, music, or dance
- Idea organizers—students map or web responses to stories
- Thinking—students daydream, stare out the window, fool around, and otherwise ponder texts
- Rehearsing—students talk with peers, sketch, or free write before a response or discussion

## Reading Aloud
### (At least once each day)
- Teacher or parent reads to class or small group—generally inspirational texts that students wouldn't pick themselves
- A variety of genres are selected, such as poetry, nonfiction, fiction
- Texts may relate to a class theme

## Language Discussions
### Less than 10% of Instructional Time
- Reading strategy lessons—using a selected, whole text to help a reader or group of readers explore a strategy
- Writing minilessons—briefly focusing on one aspect of writing, revision, or editing
- Teachable moment—focusing on a strategy for reading or writing that emerges during a learning experience
- Reading or writing conference—the teacher and student may focus briefly on a language topic
- Guided reading and writing—teacher demonstrates reading and writing with students and may focus on language topics

## Learning Language by Using Language to Learn

In this curriculum, reading and writing are not "subjects" but are the "tools" for learning. Learning experiences may focus on themes and topics related to science, social studies, literature, and fine arts. In order to engage in these themes and topics, students are compelled to use a variety of reading and writing forms, functions, and strategies. Since language is learned through meaningful use, the greatest amount of classroom time is devoted to meaningful opportunities for students to read and write.

## Reflection and Discussion to Extend Comprehension

An authentic language arts curriculum also provides time for reflection and discussion of reading and writing texts and experiences. We assume that all students are constructing meaning when they interact with texts. Students have many opportunities to express these meanings through thinking, talking, writing, reading aloud, rereading, drawing, dramatizing, dancing, and so on. These reflections focus on the concepts, meanings, and social and personal messages that students are constructing as they read and write. Reflection allows students to express and extend their responses and interpretations. At the same time, students hear and view the multiple and varied interpretations of their classmates. These opportunities for personal and social reflection expand and enhance the meanings a child constructs with a text.

## Language Lessons in a Meaningful Context

In a balanced language arts curriculum, the forms and mechanics of language are always taught within a meaningful context. Language forms and structures are introduced when they are relevant and functional to students as well. When students are writing letters to organizations asking for information about endangered species, for example, the teacher may provide information on "how to write a business letter." When a particular language form, structure, or rule is immediately relevant and meaningful to what the students are trying to do with language, then language lessons are appreciated and well received.

# Teaching Language in Context: Strategy Lessons

Within the context of an experience-based language arts curriculum, the students often become interested in *how language works*. The teacher can scaffold such inquiry with strategy lessons (or minilessons) that help students explore or understand the questions about language. For example, when a group of third graders becomes interested in using dialogue in their writing, the teacher may pull them together and provide a strategy lesson exploring the written conventions of writing dialogue. Often these lessons are spontaneous, growing out of children's reading, writing, or discussions.

## *The Teachable Moment: Spontaneous Strategy Lessons*

One group of sixth graders reading *Roll of Thunder, Hear My Cry* became interested in the Southern dialects that Mildred Taylor represents in her book. Their teacher suggested listing examples of "unfamiliar" terms and phrases for later discussion.

A second grader reading to her class in a read aloud session was stumped by an unfamiliar word. She tried the "ask the kids on the carpet" strategy, and then appealed to her teacher. Her teacher asked, "Can you think of what might make sense?" This didn't work, so the teacher suggested reading ahead and returning to the puzzling word later. This strategy was successful. In this brief exchange, all the students in this class saw three reading strategies demonstrated during the read aloud session.

Teachable moments come up all the time. A small prompt can help encourage students to pursue inquiries into language forms, processes, and strategies. These "lessons" have immediate relevance and meaning to the language learner, so they are highly likely to be integrated into the child's long-term understandings of language systems and strategies.

## *The Reading Strategy Lesson*

Sometimes a teacher observes a reader or group of readers struggling with a common aspect of reading. Rather than interrupting the reading process, the teacher later provides a focused "strategy lesson." In "The Case of the Goldfish," no one in the class could read the name *Mergatroyd.* I originally wrote this story after observing that Scott and his classmates were struggling with unfamiliar names in texts they were reading. The story helped the children explore strategies for unfamiliar names.

The "reading strategy lesson" was first described by Yetta Goodman and Carolyn Burke (see Goodman, Watson, and Burke 1996) as a way of helping students develop, recognize, and strengthen proficient reading strategies. The teacher selects or develops a *whole text* in which children can explore reading strategies in an authentic context. The text supports the reader in using and understanding specific reading strategies.

## The Reading Detective Club Cases Are Strategy Lessons

Each case provides an entire story (often a story within a story) and is designed to help students focus on one or two aspects of the reading process. In addition, the debriefing sections include additional texts, the "conversations" I hope children will read as brief plays. These dialogues introduce varied perspectives rather than one truth. Your students are invited to add their voices and perspectives as they consider each case. There are no ultimate truths or facts in language study—we each have our own beliefs and theories.

# Establishing Your Reading Detective Club

## Setting Up the Cases

The Reading Detective Club is designed to help kids discover how much linguistic knowledge they already have and to help kids build upon the most effective and efficient reading strategies. *It is absolutely essential that students work through the cases without an adult's help, so they can see the strength of their own reading and thinking processes.* It is important that students have plenty of time to "solve" the cases and talk about them informally before the debriefings.

In order to bolster self-confidence, the cases start out very easy, and grow more challenging as they go along. There are no "wrong" answers, since all answers show our thinking processes. Our job, as club sponsors, is to constantly remind students of how smart they are and how much they know. We need to create an atmosphere where students can share and explain their responses, even responses that seem unexpected or even inappropriate.

Of course, solving cases is hard work. Children who are used to assignments that are quick and easy may become frustrated. We need to provide plenty of time and encourage detectives to keep trying. Reading is not a race; it's about making meaning. The Reading Detective Club should be a fun and exciting learning experience that students look forward to.

• **Recommended ages:** The Reading Detective Club is most appropriate in grades three to six, or for eight- to twelve-year-olds in a nongraded program. Detectives must be able to read the cases without assistance from an adult. Of course, I expect the children will have miscues when they read, but the program is not recommended for beginning readers. Second- and third-grade teachers who want to try the club should be selective about which cases they introduce to their students. I would recommend that third graders start in the second semester. My biggest concern is that less able readers will conclude they are not members of the classroom literacy club. (I'm working on a Reading Detective Club for beginning readers.)

• **Before you start:** I would recommend becoming very familiar with the student book before organizing the detective club. You should work through each case yourself or with other adults. This will help you understand the focus of the case and anticipate how students may react.

• **Getting started:** I start The Reading Detective Club with a lot of ceremony. Each detective gets an invitation and a badge. Think of the atmosphere of a sailing or dancing club where club activities alternate with club meetings.

• **Preparing The Reading Detective Club cases for your students:** You have permission to copy the student pages for your students. (Please ask your colleagues to buy their own copies!) There are several ways you can use this book with your class. You might make a copy of the entire case book for each child. You can spiral-bind these books or place them in file folders and staple them in. You might copy the case and debriefing pages as separate handouts, as you use them for the detective meetings. You might copy the cases as single pages, allowing the kids to focus on solving them before moving on to the debriefing. Then you can give them the debriefing pages. Or you might go through the debriefing pages orally, only copying the sections you feel are most relevant for your class. How you copy and distribute this book to your students will depend on how you organize your club, so read on before you make any final decisions.

- **Organizing the club with your students:** The student section on "How to Use This Book" (pp. 57–59) allows you to involve students in organizing the club. Allow detective club members time to read my letter and the suggestions for The Reading Detective Club. Have club members help you decide on a plan that will work best for their Reading Detective Club. If you are working with a whole class, it might be easier to set up a planning committee.

- **Where to begin:** You can, of course, begin with "The Case of the Missing Word." Students can't believe how easy it is. This case bolsters their confidence for the more challenging cases ahead. On the other hand, I usually start with one of the investigations, such as "Easy as Falling off a Bicycle" or "What Have You Read Today?" Remember that the cases don't have to be done in order. It's up to the club members (and their sponsor) how they begin and proceed.

- **Organizing The Reading Detective Club in a classroom:** The Reading Detective Club can be organized in a number of ways. You might set up a Reading Detective Club center. A new case can be placed in the center each week or two. Students can visit the center in informal groups, pairs, or set teams. (Some cases lend themselves to small groups, while others can be done independently.) After students have all had an opportunity to solve the case, the class can come together for the "debriefing" activities. Or you can call each team together for a small group debriefing. Another Reading Detective Club option is to set aside regular times for The Reading Detective Club cases and club meetings and have the teams meet simultaneously to solve the case.

- **Organizing a Reading Detective Club in a library or reading center:** The Reading Detective Club can also be organized in a reading center or library. The group can meet at a regular time, like any school club. It would be ideal to have a small group of five to ten students. The club might be an ongoing "minicourse" so new groups get to join each quarter or semester. Another option is for the specialist to work with the classroom teacher as an additional adult sponsor for the class Reading Detective Club.

- **Organizing a Reading Detective Club at home:** Parents can establish a Reading Detective Club with their children at home. They might invite other children for a more clublike atmosphere. A mixed-age group of three to six detectives would be ideal, although children can also work alone or in pairs. Parents can allow their children and other members to work through the mystery cases independently, and then use the debriefing pages to talk about the case with the detective team.

## *Solving the Cases*

- **Introducing the cases:** Again, I suggest you start by working through each case yourself. This will help you think about how the case should be organized. There are some cases, such as "The Case of the Goldfish," that work best with teams. You might start students off with a pep talk about the case. Review the detective strategies that students have developed in previous cases. Remind students that there are no wrong answers, only good thinking.

- **Solving the cases:** Detectives should work through the cases *without adult assistance.* This is essential so that kids see their own linguistic power. In most instances, each child should work through a case alone before working it through with a detective team. It's important that each child participates in solving each mystery.

- **Detective teams:** If you're working with a small group (five to ten), everyone is a member of the detective team. In a large class, students can be organized into teams of three or four (or up to five, if your class is really large). Teams might choose a name and decorate a folder for team materials, and so forth. Gentle competition adds to the mystique, and children work harder to solve each case. However, make sure students understand that the goal is to solve the case—and not to finish first.

- **Group process:** Take time to talk about "what went well" for each group after a case. This will help bring out the give and take of small-group learning. It's important that *every child* participates in solving each mystery case. In order to encourage full participation, teams can reach consensus in coming up with solutions or debriefing reports. With consensus, each child is asked by the team whether they agree or disagree with each point during team debriefings.

### When Detectives "Get Stuck"

Detectives will come to unknown or unfamiliar text besides the "missing words." They will also find some cases very challenging, and may feel they can't solve them. Resist the temptation to provide answers or even suggestions or hints, but remind readers to use their smart detective strategies. If we help kids read the text or solve the case directly, we are taking away their opportunity to think for themselves. Remember that you will be able to talk about responses and provide hints and suggestions during the debriefings. Here are some suggestions for encouraging independent work:

- Be patient and resist requests for help. Tell students they have all the time in the world to work things out. Reading is not a race. Keep trying.

## Becoming Learning Detectives

There are many parallels between learning to read and learning in general. The investigation "Easy as Falling off a Bike" explores the relationship between reading and learning. Reading detectives can easily identify parallels between reading and other language or thinking processes. Readers predict while mathematicians estimate, scientists form hypotheses, and so on. Reading detectives might become interested in exploring related issues in other areas of the curriculum.

• Have detectives treat unknown words or unfamiliar text as part of the mystery and use their strategies to work it out themselves. They can even cross out the trouble spot in order to focus on story meaning and context.

• Remind students that they are the smart detectives who can solve the case for themselves. There are no right answers, just good thinking.

• Remind readers to use detective strategies that the class has worked out, such as reading ahead or rereading. You might review your class list of strategies before each case begins.

• As the cases get more difficult, students will need to read the text several times in order to come up with likely responses. Tell them to keep trying. Encourage them to brainstorm and make guesses.

• Encourage students to come up with responses that make sense even if they don't exactly fit with the clues in the case. If they can't find one word to fit a "missing word" slot, they might think of a phrase that makes sense. Their responses don't have to rhyme or include the right letters; they just have to make sense. Once they've thought of a meaningful response, they can go back and consider other possible responses.

• Some readers may get easily frustrated or upset. Try pairing them up with other detectives for the initial read through. Pair up kids who will support each other without one child supplying all of the reading or responses. It might be better to pair up readers with similar capabilities, rather than pairing a highly proficient reader with a less proficient reader.

• Once students or pairs have done all they can on their own, they can share their answers with other members of their detective team.

## Debriefings

The purpose of the debriefings is to help detectives organize and explore their new understandings about the reading process. The debriefing activities and "conversations" bring up some of the issues introduced by a detective case. The debriefing pages are meant to *facilitate* debriefing discussions. But the discussions should highlight the thoughts and reflections of *your* club members. *It's important that the debriefing activities do not become written busywork.* Teams might select scribes and read the questions and discuss responses rather than always writing out their answers.

Here are some tips for debriefing sessions:

• **Share diverse responses:** Start by having students share responses so they can see all of the possible interpretations detectives might have. Do not comment on the appropriateness of any responses, but allow students to explore the thinking processes that these responses reveal.

• **Value every response:** The goal is to "revalue" reading, so we begin by placing value on each child's thinking. Children's responses may be unexpected, or they may change the meaning of a text. However, they are never random. We need to point out to club members how responses are cued by the language systems. If a child provides an unexpected response, help the child explain his or her thinking process to the class. It's important to focus on the linguistic knowledge the child used to come up with the response, rather than the appropriateness of the response. It's particularly important for the teacher to explore the value of a child's response if the child's first

### Becoming Reading Detectives During Reading Times

The Reading Detective Club activities and discussions transfer very easily to other reading and writing experiences. Teachers can encourage students to use their club strategies during independent reading, reading across the curriculum, and all other classroom reading. Parents can encourage their children to ask themselves "what makes sense" and use the strategies when reading at home. Detectives will notice investigations everywhere as they approach a variety of texts and reading experiences. Encourage and assist children in pursuing these investigations—and please send them to me in case I write the sequel: MORE Reading Detective Club mysteries.

language is not English or if the child speaks a dialect different from the teacher or other class members.

- **Follow the detectives' leads:** If children bring up issues other than those I have included in the debriefing pages, encourage them to follow up on these issues. *If any of the debriefing activities become tedious, boring, or irrelevant to your Reading Detective Club,* please *skip them, adapt them, or abandon them!*

- **Enjoy the conversations:** Your children might enjoy performing the conversations as short plays. Children might rehearse a conversation and present it to the entire group at the appropriate time. Or detective team members can each take a role and read the conversations informally.

## Evaluation

The Reading Detective Club cases provide excellent activities for evaluation of student progress in reading. Be sure to collect and review individual student responses to each detective case. These responses will help you see which students have strong independent reading strategies, which students struggle to make guesses, and which students appear to be losing meaning as they read.

The student reflections also help teachers get a sense of how students view the reading process and themselves as readers. The accumulated set of cases provides a record of how students' views and understandings progress. The reflections are a valuable record of student growth in understanding the reading process. Reviewing the student responses to the cases should also inform instruction. Teachers might return to specific cases or strategies, provide small-group strategy lessons, or provide individual assistance depending on readers' responses during the cases.

## Grading

Frank Smith (1988) has said that you can't invite kids to join the Literacy Club and then grade them for it. I share his concern. What message does it give kids to know they are an "*A* reader" or a "*D* reader," or a "satisfactory reader" or an "unsatisfactory reader"? My son had a wonderful third-grade teacher who encouraged him to become interested in reading and writing for the first time since he had started school. However, when he received a *C* in reading on his report card, his interest and effort dropped rapidly.

Yet, most of us are required to give grades. One option is not to grade The Reading Detective Club because of the complex implications. And that might be a viable option, considering that it is a club. However,

I feel kids should "get credit" for all of their reading. Also what we grade tells kids *what we value.* So my approach is that all club members "get credit" for their hard work and effort in The Reading Detective Club—members get credit for participating in cases and discussion. However, The Reading Detective Club credit only helps them earn "good grades" in reading, because my goal is to prove that all kids are good readers!

# Overview of
# the Reading Detective Club Cases

## *Part One: Reading Detectives Use Clues and Strategies*

The cases in Part One introduce three kinds of clues readers use: meaning clues, language clues, and graphic clues.

"The Case of the Missing Word" (p. 63). Removing the graphic cues in the first few cases forces readers to rely on other cueing systems. This story and debriefings focus on "meaning clues" and our meaning-making strategies. This case is also designed to be "easy" and provides a successful first experience, demonstrating to children that they are skilled language users.

"The Case of the Messy Hands" (p. 67). Once again, readers are forced to use meaning and language cues rather than to focus on surface features. This case has ten "missing words" rather than one, so children learn to work through a more complex text without becoming discouraged. However, the familiar story ("The Three Little Pigs") provides a strong support for children to be successful. This case inevitably leads to a variety of responses, helping children see that readers interpret texts differently (but there are no wrong answers).

The reflection pages focus on "language clues" as children talk explicitly about concepts they already understand intuitively, such as adjectives and nouns.

"The Case of the Torn Page" (p. 72). In this case, graphophonic cues are added, as well as rhyming clues. This information makes the case a little more difficult, especially if children try to use semantic and syntactic strategies AND the letters and rhymes. The focus on meaning making already established should encourage students to come up with a "best guess." The reflection pages introduce the concept of letter or graphic clues and their role in the reading process.

"The Case of the Gluey Page (p. 76). I threw this one in because my Aunt Shirley, who read an early version of this book, suggested that children like to do something again once they know how to do it. You will find that I use this motto throughout the book.

EXTENDING: CLOZE PROCEDURES  You may find that children enjoy this type of "mystery," which borrows from cloze procedures. You and your students can create additional stories for your detective club center. An easy way is to take a short story and "smudge out" selected words. I suggest five to ten "smudges" since more spaces are too much for discussion.

I have also used a modified cloze procedure as a type of miscue analysis. This process is described in detail in my chapter in *The Whole Language Evaluation Book* (Goodman 1989).

## Part Two: Let's Take a Guess!

Now that we've introduced three kinds of language clues, we move on to focus on language strategies.

"The Case of the Goldfish" (p. 81). This case focuses on "making predictions," helping children understand that readers are always making predictions when we read. Also, when children focus *consciously* on making predictions about the story, they become more active in seeking text cues to support their predictions. As they continue to read, they actively seek additional cues to confirm or disconfirm their predictions. This process of predicting and confirming helps students become aware of the reading process when they talk about the case during the debriefing.

The actual story focuses on the specific strategy of dealing with an unfamiliar name. When children report their own difficulties with texts, they frequently involve unfamiliar names. Although there is no problem in *understanding* the text (since the children know the word is a name), children often get stuck trying to *pronounce* the name. This case provides several strategies for this common "reading problem." In addition, the discussion will help children see that other readers in their class—even the most proficient ones—come across puzzling or unfamiliar texts when they read.

EXTENDING PREDICTION: DIRECTED READING THINKING ACTIVITY (DRTA)  You may recognize the process I used in this case, often called DRTA. This approach can be used for "guided reading" experiences with a variety of stories and books. It can be used during read aloud (as a listening activity), or as a silent reading experience (as in "The Case of the Goldfish"). This procedure helps children bring their experiences and schema to reading a text and actively search for cues to assist in predicting and confirming strategies. I would use the DRTA sparingly, and particularly with stories with surprise endings. The process does interrupt the story and may get tiring if overused.

## Part Three: Everybody Makes Mistakes

In this section, reading detectives learn that mistakes, or *miscues,* are an important aspect of reading and writing. They learn reading focuses on "meaning construction" rather than on accuracy or correctness.

"The Case of the Missing Mom" (p. 95). The story "Is Your Mom at Home?" is a rip-off of a story Ken Goodman (1996) wrote called "A Boat in the Basement." These stories prove to readers that we don't read letter by letter or word by word. Instead, readers sample cues selectively as they construct meaning with a text. One of the most amazing things about this case is that we notice some of the smaller typos while we miss some of the biggest ones. I gave away the example of *ice creem* because that is one you are likely to notice. Another is the substitution of *hume* for *home.* In each case, only one letter has been changed. However, these words are concept carriers for the story, and so we probably look at them more closely.

One of the last things that readers usually notice is the insertion of extra words. (Did you find the double words?) Our mind absolutely rejects seeing the same information twice. It is extremely rare for anyone to find all of the mistakes in this text, even after several readings, though a group working together stands a better chance. After writing this story, I had difficulty finding all the changes I had made.

Again, the main point here is that we read with a focus on meaning, and we do not *perceive* all of the surface features. I also use this story to help kids begin to see that miscues are part of the process of reading and writing. They are not a big deal. But, more important, they give evidence of how we think. In addition, human beings have an incredible capacity for making meaning, accommodating and "correcting" these miscues as we go.

"The Case of the Damaged Books" (p. 101). Since readers enjoy "The Case of the Missing Mom," I have the children "write" their own cases. This gives detectives a chance to try their proofreading skills again and find all the hidden typos. Of course, nobody's perfect, so Michele also includes a few unintentional mistakes. Here readers can continue to see that mistakes are a part of the meaning-construction process, whether they are the writer or the reader.

"The Case of the Smashed Chicken" (p. 103). Again, Jacob's case gives reading detectives an opportunity to try a strategy that they have used already. Jacob's and Michele's stories also set the stage for your students to write their own stories with planted errors and to look for interesting typos in texts they are reading. Once again, Jacob has a few unintentional miscues.

"The Kas of the Stoopid Chekin" (p. 105). When I realized that Scott, my first-grade character, was going to write a story I could not resist the opportunity to explore invented spellings. The story gives young readers a chance to start thinking about the role of miscues in writing as well as reading. While experienced writers all make "miscues" of the type in "Is Your Mom at Home?," beginning writers often produce "miscues" that look like Scott's. The reflection pages encourage kids to "translate" Scott's story. This may help them to be more appreciative and tolerant readers of their classmates' writings, as well as that of younger children.

As children work through the reflection pages, they may notice some of the patterns in Scott's spelling. This story is a sham, since it was not written by a six-year-old, but I based Scott's spellings on beginning writers I have worked with. Scott's spellings show what he knows about language, and might be interesting to explore with your students. For example, it is common for children to spell the /I/ sound in "chicken" with an *e*, because /I/ is actually closer to the sound of the letter *e* than it is to sound of the letter *i*.

Scott's spelling mistakes provide several patterns for discussion.

- He spells phonetically in many cases, representing how words sound to him: cheki**nz, wuz, famus, truk**
- Within these phonetic spellings there are patterns. For example, Scott uses vowels in all syllables except those with *r*: *frm, navr,* and so on. This is because *r* tends to control the sounds of the vowels around it.
- He also knows some conventional spelling patterns. For example, the *oo* in k**oo**d is based on words like *book* or *good*. Another example is *leev*. He also knows that the single sound at the beginning of *chicken* is represented with two letters, *ch,* as is the single sound at the beginning of *the*.
- As Jacob points out in the conversation, Scott also spells many words conventionally.

Your students may enjoy investigating invented spellings of beginning writers. Investigation #4 (page 166) provides direction for a study of invented spellings.

## Part Four: Playing with Language

These cases focus on the syntactic cueing system (or language clues). Nonsense words replace all of the content words (nouns, verbs, adjectives, and adverbs) in the text. This deprives readers of semantic cues (meaning clues) and helps them to see how we use our intuitive understanding of language structure when we read. I also poke fun at standardized tests, while at the same time give detectives some strategies for taking comprehension tests.

"The Case of the Norful Snig" (p. 115). Here children are denied the semantic cues needed to construct meaning with the text. The "comprehension questions" allow children to see how they use their knowledge of "language clues" when they read. Children may become frustrated by the nonsense words. This is good—*we want children to be intolerant of nonsense in text!* But the "detective" tact should encourage children to work at answering the questions. As they bring their understandings of language patterns and transformations (from statement to question) to solving the case, they will realize what smart kids they are! Resist helping them too much, though you might go over the tips with them.

After answering the nonsense questions, children create a story using "The Norful Snig" as a code. Now they are able to bring meaning to unfamiliar text. This case obviously has implications for testing as well as for reading. As detectives, children are learning they can consciously manipulate the language of texts and apply "code-breaking" strategies to unfamiliar words or phrases. We can use this to develop test-taking strategies, but also to recognize what it means to be a reader. There is an obvious difference between reading tests and actual reading.

"The Shrag of the Glumpy Frinkle" (p. 124). Of course, Michele, Jacob, and Scott have to take a turn at writing their own nonsense story. This allows your students to practice the syntactic strategies they developed to solve "The Case of the Norful Snig." It also allows you to extend the debriefing discussion. If you focused on syntactic cues in the last case, you might focus the debriefing on test-taking strategies for this case.

CREATING YOUR OWN NONSENSE STORIES   These stories are created by substituting nonsense words for most *content words* (nouns, verbs, adjectives, and adverbs). The function words (determiners, prepositions, possessives) remain to maintain the syntactic structure of the English language. We use the story as a code because the substituted words are used consistently throughout the story. In addition, we use conventional structures for plurals, possessives, and verb tenses. So *Mary has two brothers. The oldest brother is John.* becomes *Mishuganah has splunk plinkers. The shvinkest plinker is John.* This would be a great time to read Lewis Carroll's "Jabberwocky."

## Part Five: You Are What You Read, or You Read What You Are

In this section, children learn that we must bring meaning to the text in order to construct meaning with the text. Reading detectives explore how schema and prior experiences influence reading. They learn that reading is a constant process of interpreting texts as we construct them.

There are many areas for discussion around these cases. We can talk about what makes reading "easy" as children come to understand that texts are "easy" if we have knowledge or experience with a topic. We can talk about how reading involves "understanding concepts" rather than "knowing words." We can talk about the connection between our experiences and making predictions. We extend the discussion into writing as we talk more explicitly about what it means to use concept words and provide details when we write.

"The Case of the Missing Titles" (p. 133). When the children first read Jimmy's story, they will find it very puzzling or confusing if they don't realize it's about shoveling snow. Lashanda's story will be easier to read for children who play soccer.

Have children share their ideas of what they think the stories are about before going on to the debriefing pages. Encourage them to retell as much as they can. Once children realize the topic is "shoveling snow" (because a detective guesses or because they read the debriefing pages), they should go back and reread the story.

These stories explore "schema," or the concepts and understandings we bring to texts when we read. Once we know we are reading about "shoveling snow," we activate the "shoveling snow" schema in our heads that helps us to make sense of the text. When the children talk about the stories once they know the topic, they will probably remember a lot more of the text details. Their retellings may provide language and details that are not in the text. You might use these details to point out that readers make inferences and bring meaning to the text.

The Case of My Own Miscue" (p. 140). This case allows readers to explore miscues and engage in a form of miscue analysis. Miscues are discussed in detail earlier in this text. The reader-selected miscue procedure, outlined in this case, was developed by Dorothy Watson. It is described in more detail in the book *Retrospective Miscue Analysis* (Goodman and Marek 1996).

# Recommended Reading

Brown, J., K. Goodman, and A. Marek. 1996. *Studies in Miscue Analysis: An Annotated Bibliography.* Newark, DE: International Reading Association.

Cambourne, B. 1988. *The Whole Story: Natural Learning and the Acquisition of Literacy in the Classroom.* New York: Scholastic.

Freeman, Y., and D. Freeman. 1992. *Whole Language for Second Language Learners.* Portsmouth, NH: Heinemann.

Goodman, D. 1996. "The Reading Detective Club." In *Retrospective Miscue Analysis: Revaluing Readers and Reading,* edited by Y. Goodman and A. Marek. Katonah, NY: Richard C. Owen.

——. 1989. "So Why Don't I Feel Good About Myself?" In *The Whole Language Evaluation Book,* edited by K. Goodman, Y. Goodman, and W. J. Hood. Portsmouth, NH: Heinemann.

Goodman, K. 1996. *On Reading.* Portsmouth, NH: Heinemann.

——. 1993. *Phonics Phacts.* Portsmouth, NH: Heinemann.

——. 1986. *What's Whole in Whole Language?* Portsmouth, NH: Heinemann.

Goodman, K., Y. Goodman, and W. J. Hood, eds. 1989. *The Whole Language Evaluation Book.* Portsmouth, NH: Heinemann.

Goodman, Y., and A. Marek, eds. 1996. *Retrospective Miscue Analysis.* Katonah, NY: Richard C. Owen.

Goodman, Y., D. Watson, and C. Burke. 1996. *Reading Strategies: Focus on Comprehension.* 2d ed. Katonah, NY: Richard C. Owen.

——. 1987. *Reading Miscue Inventory: Alternative Procedures.* Katonah, NY: Richard C. Owen.

Graves, D. 1991. *Build a Literate Classroom.* Portsmouth, NH: Heinemann.

——. 1990. *Discover Your Own Literacy.* Portsmouth, NH: Heinemann.

Smith, F. 1988. *Joining the Literacy Club: Further Essays into Education.* Portsmouth, NH: Heinemann.

Smith, K. 1995. "Bringing Children and Literature Together in the Elementary Classroom." *Primary Voices K-6* 3 (April).

Watson, D., and S. Hoge. 1996. "Reader Selected Miscues." *In Retrospective Miscue Analysis: Revaluing Readers and Reading,* edited by Y. Goodman and A. Marek. Katonah, NY: Richard C. Owen.

# The Reading
# Detective Club

## A Non-workbook for Junior Detectives

# *Welcome to the Reading Detective Club*

You are now an official reading-detective-in-training, but when you finish this book you will be ready to receive your detective badge. Good luck with your important cases.

## *We Are All Reading Detectives!*

When we read, we are just like detectives:
- We use clues from the author's words or printed text.
- We use clues from our own minds.
- We are always making guesses about what comes next.
- We make up theories about what we are reading as we go along.
- We use clues to see if our guesses and theories make sense.

This is not a workbook. This is a fun book. This is also a think book. This is a book to help you see how smart you already are. This is a book to let you learn some things grown-up reading detectives have found out about reading.

This book is for:
- Kids who hate workbooks, OR . . .
- Kids who like puzzles or mysteries, OR . . .
- Kids who love to read and write and think, OR . . .
- Kids who think they're not good readers, OR . . .
- Kids who like learning things, OR . . .
- Kids just like YOU!

This book will not necessarily make you a better reader. The *best* way to become a *better* reader is to *read, read, read.* (So tell your teacher and parents to give you plenty of time to read books you like.) But this book will help you solve the mystery of what makes kids good readers.

# *Letter from the Author*

*Dear Kids,*

*Hi. I'm the person who wrote this book. I put in all those big ORs . . . on the page you just read because I like having choices, don't you? This book is to have fun with, so don't worry about doing it in the right order. Don't worry about getting the answers right. There are no right answers. Make sure your teacher and parents know that <u>only you</u> can decide if your answers are right or if you want to change them.*

*You might find some hard parts while you're trying to solve the detective cases. I put those parts in on purpose. But don't worry. <u>Cheating is allowed in this club</u>. In fact, it's encouraged. We learn best when we work together. So look at your friends' answers. Talk the cases over with your parents and teachers and other good readers you know.*

*But remember, <u>you</u> are the detective. It's up to you to decide if you've solved the mystery. There are no answer sheets, because there are no right answers. Just keep your mind open for clues and have fun.*

*This is <u>your</u> club.*

*Love,*

*Debi Goodman*

*P. S. I'm actually writing on my computer, but I'm using a kind of type, or "font," that makes it look like handwriting. When you see this font, you will know that it's me—the author—talking to you—the detective. Good luck!*

*P. P. S. If you really enjoy detective work, you might want to look for other examples of how I used different fonts or formats to make this book easier to understand or more interesting to read.*

# *Contents*

## 4

### Playing with Language

## 5

### You Are What You Read, or You Read What You Are

### Investigations

# *How to Use This Book*

## *1. Start a Reading Detective Club*

This book contains mystery cases. The mysteries are much more fun to solve with a group of friends. You will also learn more if you share ideas. Get some friends to join your club and go through the book together. If you're in a large group (like a class), divide into little clubs. Your club will work best if you have three or four detectives. If you don't have two friends to work with, one will be fine.

## *2. Take Your Time*

Each case is a puzzle for you to solve. The puzzles are thinking puzzles, which means it will take you some *time* to solve each one. *You should plan to do just one puzzle at each club meeting.* The important thing about solving mysteries is to be *thoughtful,* not to be fast. If you are working in a group, some people will solve the mystery more quickly than others, but the first people done won't necessarily have the best solutions (answers).

## *3. Use the Reflection Pages*

Each mystery case is followed by *debriefing* activities to help your club think about the mystery that you've just solved. *Debriefing is when detectives interrogate (question) each other in order to discover new information.* The reflection pages will help you think about *what* you've discovered and *how* you made those discoveries, so you can become *master detectives. You don't have to do all of the reflection pages.* OR . . . if you get tired of writing everything down, you might want to use the reflection questions just to talk about what you learned. You might think of your own activities or debriefings. The reflection pages are just there to help you think about what you've learned and become better detectives.

## 4. Choose Your Cases, But Don't Spoil the Mystery

You don't have to work on the cases in order. You can look through the book and pick cases that look fun or interesting to you. Be careful if you skim through the book. There are some cases that will be spoiled if you read them ahead of time. I have put warnings on these cases so you don't read them accidentally.

## 5. Have Fun!

Besides the detective cases, there are some conversations in the reflection sections. You might want to read these out loud like a play.

## 6. Take a Look at the Investigations

At the end of the book, there are some invitations for other investigations your club might try. These invitations might take time and involve home detective work, so you may want to look at them now and mark the ones you may be interested in.

## Suggestions for Your Detective Club Meetings

- Plan to meet once or twice a week for about thirty to sixty minutes.

- It might be fun if a teacher or club member tells a little about the day's case in order to build up the suspense.

- Have enough copies of the mystery for each club member. Let the club members work on the mystery alone for a while before comparing answers. You might want to have a separate time to work on cases *before* your club meeting.

- There are usually two debriefings after each mystery. You might do one activity right after you solve the mystery, and do the other activity at the start of the next meeting. If you meet twice a week, you could use one meeting for solving a case and the other for a debriefing.

- Be flexible. Remember, the goal is to think and talk about reading.

## Possible Agendas for Your Reading Detective Meetings

**Meeting Agenda
(45 to 60 minutes)**
*(Once a week)*

1. Go over the agenda for today.*

2. Hold a debriefing on the last mystery case.*

3. Complete the second reflection activity on the last case.

4. Work on today's mystery case.

5. Complete the first reflection activity on the case.

6. Hold a debriefing discussion.*

**Meeting Agenda
(30 to 45 minutes)**
*(Twice a week)*

***Meeting One: The Case***
1. Go over the agenda for today.*

2. Work on today's mystery case.

3. Complete the first reflection activity on the case.

***Meeting Two: The Debriefing***
1. Go over the agenda for today.*

2. Hold a discussion about the case.*

3. Complete the second reflection activity.

4. Hold a debriefing discussion.*

*If you have many clubs in your class, you might do these parts together.

*Okay! Ready for your first case? Turn the page for . . . "The Case of the Missing Word."*

© 1999 by Debra Goodman.
From The Reading Detective
Club. Portsmouth, NH:
Heinemann.

# 1

# Reading Detectives Use Clues and Strategies

# The Case of the Missing Word

Jacob is a famous detective. He had solved many important cases.

One day, Michele came to see Jacob. She said, "I have a case for you."

Jacob said, "What is it?"

Michele showed Jacob a book. She said, "I wanted to read my book, but my dumb brother crossed out some words. Now I can't read it. Can you help me?"

Jacob said, "Did your brother say anything about the words?"

"Yes," Michele said, "He said it is the same word over and over. He said it is a word he doesn't like."

Jacob read the book. He said, "I think I can solve this case."

Here is a page from Michele's book:

> Hi. My name is Jim.
> I have one brother and one xxxxxx.
> My brother is Sam. My xxxxxx is Lisa.
> I am ten years old, and my brother is twelve.
> My xxxxxx is just a baby. She is two.
> I like my brother, but my xxxxxx can be a real pest.

**HINT!**

The number of *x* marks has nothing to do with the number of letters in the missing word.

What is the missing word? _____

© 1999 by Debra Goodman.
*From* The Reading Detective
Club. *Portsmouth, NH:
Heinemann.*

# DEBRIEFING:
# The Case of the Missing Word

## *Reading Detectives Use <u>Clues</u> When They Read*

*Congratulations on solving your first case! Jacob (and you) couldn't use letter clues to figure out the missing word. You had to think about <u>what makes sense</u> in the story. Go back to the story and underline the <u>clues</u> that helped you figure out the missing word.*

*What clues helped you figure out the missing word?*

_____

_____

_____

_____

_____

_____

_____

_____

_____

_____

_____

_____

**WHAT'S THE BIG IDEA?**

**Meaning clues are the most important clues that reading detectives use, because reading is a way to understand the meaning of the text. When we use meaning clues, we are trying to answer the question: What makes sense?**

*Share your clues with your friends and talk about <u>why</u> these clues helped you figure out the missing word. We call these clues <u>meaning clues</u>, because they help us work out the meaning of the missing word.*

*© 1999 by Debra Goodman. From* The Reading Detective Club. *Portsmouth, NH: Heinemann.*

## *Reading Detectives Use <u>Strategies</u> When They Read*

JACOB: When I saw the first xxxxxxx, I went back and read the sentence again. I read the word *brother* and guessed that the next word was *sister.*

MICHELE: At first I thought the missing word was *nephew.* I have one brother and one *nephew.* Then I saw the sentence "My xxxxxxx is Lisa." And the sentence, "She is two." I knew it must be a girl. So I changed my answer to *niece.*

*Jacob <u>rereads</u> to pick up the pattern "brother and sister." Michele predicts <u>nephew</u> and then <u>reads ahead</u> for more clues.*

*Detectives: What were you thinking as you were reading and trying to solve this case? What strategies did you use?*

_____

_____

_____

_____

_____

_____

_____

_____

_____

_____

*Share your strategies with your club members. You might want to start a chart listing reading detective strategies and add to it after each case. There is a chart on page 78 you can use.*

© 1999 by Debra Goodman. *From* The Reading Detective Club. *Portsmouth, NH: Heinemann.*

## Conversation

JACOB: Hey, what's the difference between a clue and a strategy?

MICHELE: Well, I guess a clue is *what* you notice about the book or magazine or whatever that helps you read. And a strategy is *how* the detective thinks about the clues.

JACOB: Yeah! So the clues are in the story and the strategies are in the detective. That means it takes books and brains to make sense when you're reading.

MICHELE: You're right! The book doesn't make any sense without the reader.

### A Strategy Tip

DETECTIVES: *Now that you know how to solve "The Case of the Missing Word," you can use the same strategies when you read.*

*When you are reading and you come to a word or phrase that is confusing or unfamiliar, pretend it is "a missing word." Say "blank" and use your strategies to figure out what makes sense just like you did with "The Case of the Missing Word."*

*How'd you do on your first case?*
*Too easy? Ready for something more difficult? Here comes . . . "The Case of the Messy Hands."*

**WHAT'S THE BIG IDEA?**

**A written text\* has meaning clues. But a reading detective has to <u>interpret</u> the meaning clues to make sense. <u>Interpret</u> means that the detective uses the meaning clues to <u>make meaning</u> with a text. It takes a reader or a writer to make a meaningful text. <u>Reading is making meaning.</u>**

**DETECTIVES: The word "text" means the printed writing on a page. It's a useful word if you want to include all printed writing, such as stories, newspapers, signs, and so on.**

*© 1999 by Debra Goodman. From* The Reading Detective Club. *Portsmouth, NH: Heinemann.*

# The Case of the Messy Hands

Jacob was a famous detective. One day Michele stormed into Jacob's office shouting, "My stupid brother has done it again!"

Jacob asked, "What is it this time? Did he cross out some more words in your book?"

"No," said Michele, "This time he wanted to read my book. But he never washes his hands. Every time he touched my book with his grubby paws, he smudged up the words so I can't read them."

"Let me take a look," Jacob said. "I'll see what I can do."

Michele handed Jacob the book.

Jacob said, "I think I can solve this case."

Psst: Work by yourself before you compare answers.

**HINT!**
If you can't think of a good guess for one of the smudges, keep reading. When you have read the whole story, go back and try again. Try to come up with a word that makes sense for each smudge.

THE THREE LITTLE PIGS

Once upon a  there were three little pigs.

One day the  pigs decided to go out into the

world to make their  .

Each little pig  a house.

The first little pig built a house of  .

The  little pig built a house of sticks.

The third little pig built a  of bricks.

One  a wolf saw the three little pigs.

"A little  will make a tasty meal for me,"

he  .

Your solutions:

1. _____

2. _____

3. _____

4. _____

5. _____

6. _____

7. _____

8. _____

9. _____

10. _____

67

© 1999 by Debra Goodman. From The Reading Detective Club. Portsmouth, NH: Heinemann.

# DEBRIEFING:
# The Case of the Messy Hands

*Readers Have Different Interpretations*
*When They Read*

*Congratulations on solving your second case! If you are working with*
*a group of friends, take a look at some of your friends' answers for each*  *.*
*Use this chart to compare your answers.*

| Number | My Answer | Friends' Answers | Clues We Used to Get Answers |
|---|---|---|---|
| 1. | _____ | _____ | _____ |
| 2. | _____ | _____ | _____ |
| 3. | _____ | _____ | _____ |
| 4. | _____ | _____ | _____ |
| 5. | _____ | _____ | _____ |
| 6. | _____ | _____ | _____ |
| 7. | _____ | _____ | _____ |
| 8. | _____ | _____ | _____ |
| 9. | _____ | _____ | _____ |
| 10. | _____ | _____ | _____ |

## Playing Around with Language
### Conversation

JACOB: Hey, we got different answers. Look at number two. I put "three pigs" and you put "little pigs." Which one is right?

MICHELE: Well, the story is called "The Three Little Pigs." Both of our answers make sense.

JACOB: I guess we're both right. The author could have written lots of things—like "fat pigs."

MICHELE: Or "silly pigs."

JACOB: Or "busy pigs."

DETECTIVES: *How many words can you think of that would make sense*

*or the smudge in "the*  *pigs"?*

fat _____ _____ _____ _____

silly _____ _____ _____ _____

busy _____ _____ _____ _____

_____ _____ _____ _____

*All of the words on this list describe the pigs. Language detectives (linguists) call these words adjectives. If you said, "the table pigs" or "the when pigs," it just wouldn't sound right, would it? When we read, we use the whole sentence to know what kind of word goes into each blank space. When we find the right kind of word to fit each smudge, we are using language clues. In this sentence, the language clues actually force us to choose adjectives. Nothing else sounds right.*

### Conversation

MICHELE: Boy, I never heard of adjectives, but I know what they are somehow!

JACOB: This sounds stupid, but at first I didn't think of an adjective. I just wrote *pigs*—"One day the *pigs* decided"—I didn't even notice that it already said *pigs* until I went back and read it again. I guess I just wasn't thinking.

MICHELE: Why do you say you weren't thinking? When you read "One

© *1999 by Debra Goodman.*
*From* The Reading Detective
Club. *Portsmouth, NH:*
*Heinemann.*

day the" you know it's talking about pigs. You were using language clues, but you were using meaning clues, too.

JACOB: Hey, you're right. You know, I AM a great detective. I just realized you can even leave the adjective out of the sentence. It would still mean the same if you just said, "One day the pigs decided to go out into the world."

MICHELE: You're right, I wonder why we need adjectives, anyway?

JACOB: Well, maybe they make the story more interesting. They help me make pictures of the story in my head.

MICHELE: And, they do give you more information. It would change the meaning if the story said "the stupid pigs" or "the smart pigs," wouldn't it?

JACOB: Playing around with language is fun.

MICHELE: Let's think of some funny words for the sentence "The first little pig built a house of *smudge*." How about mud?

JACOB: How about Legos?

DETECTIVES: *What funny words can you think of for "house of*  *"?*

mud _____ _____ _____ _____

Legos _____ _____ _____ _____

_____ _____ _____ _____

_____ _____ _____ _____

*Did you think of as many words for this smudge as you could for the adjective smudge? All these words are called* <u>nouns</u>. *They are all words that stand for "things." But in this sentence, the nouns also have to be building materials. In fact, in "The Three Little Pigs," this word has to be something like* <u>straw</u> *or* <u>hay</u>. *Any other words would change the story meaning.*

© 1999 by Debra Goodman. *From* The Reading Detective Club. *Portsmouth, NH: Heinemann.*

**WHAT'S THE BIG IDEA?**

**Even if you've never heard the word <u>adjectives</u> before, your brain knows when you need to use an adjective. You are using <u>language clues</u> when you read. Language clues help us put words together into sentences that make sense. Language clues answer the questions "What sounds right?" or "What sounds like language?"**

## Conversation

MICHELE: I think nouns must be more important than adjectives. You can't leave out the word *straw*. The story wouldn't make sense at all if you didn't know that the first little pig didn't make a very strong house.

JACOB: Hey, you're right. Words like *house* and *bricks* are very important. But words like *little* aren't very important. What about *the* and *of*?

MICHELE: Yeah. Look at the sentence: "The first little pig built a house of straw."

JACOB: Lots of extra words. First pig built house straw. The rest just take up space.

MICHELE: It sure sounds funny, but you don't have to talk out loud when you're reading, do you? You can understand the sentence with just about half of the words. Hey! Maybe that's why I can read to myself faster than I can read a story out loud.

JACOB: I sure wish I'd gotten into the reading detective business sooner. I always thought that good readers had to know *all* the words. Now we find out that some words are more important, and some words don't matter much at all.

### A Strategy Tip

*Here's a fun reading strategy. When you're reading, and you come to something that confuses you, pretend it's a smudge. Think of all the words that might make sense. Then decide which one sounds best.*

*Okay—we talked about meaning clues and language clues. What do you suppose comes next? You're about to find out. It's . . .*
*"The Case of the Torn Page"!!!!*

**WHAT'S THE BIG IDEA?**
**Some words are more important than other words. Good reading means "making sense," not "getting the words right."**

*© 1999 by Debra Goodman. From* The Reading Detective Club. *Portsmouth, NH: Heinemann.*

# The Case of the Torn Page

Jacob was a famous detective. He had solved many important cases. One day Michele came to see Jacob. She was holding a book.

"Not again!" Jacob said. "What did your brother do this time?"

Michele shook her head sadly. "This case may be too hard for you," she said.

Jacob said, "*No* case is too hard for me. Tell me what happened."

Michele said, "Well. I was reading my book and my horrible brother tried to grab it right out of my hands. I held onto the book, but he tore one of the pages."

"Let me see the book," Jacob said.

Michele opened her book to the torn page. She said, "Most of the sentences are missing the last word."

Jacob looked at the torn page. "This may take time," he said. "But I think I can solve this case."

Here is Michele's book:

## TEN LITTLE SQUIRRELS

Ten little squirrels played in a tree.
The first one said, "What do I see?
The second one said, "A man with a
The third one said, "We'd better ru
The fourth one said, "Let's hide in the s
The fifth one said, "I'm not afraid.
The sixth one said, "Don't make a sound.
The seventh one said, "He's looking all
The eighth one said, "Let's run to our n
The ninth one said, "No staying here is
The tenth one sneezed . . .
    "Ker. . . ker. . . ker. . . ker. . . KERCHOO!"
Then BANG went the gun,
And ten little squirrels, how they did

1. _____
2. _____
3. _____

4. _____
5. _____
6. _____

7. _____

# DEBRIEFING:
# The Case of the Torn Page

*What clues helped you to solve "The Case of the Torn Page"?*

_____

_____

_____

_____

_____

_____

_____

*Would you like to compare your answers with your friends' again? You can use this chart:*

|  | **My Answer** | **Friends' Answers** | **Clues We Used to Get Answers** |
|---|---|---|---|
| 1. | _____ | _____ | _____ |
| 2. | _____ | _____ | _____ |
| 3. | _____ | _____ | _____ |
| 4. | _____ | _____ | _____ |
| 5. | _____ | _____ | _____ |
| 6. | _____ | _____ | _____ |
| 7. | _____ | _____ | _____ |

## Reading Detectives Use Graphic/Phonics Clues as well as Language and Meaning Clues

In "The Case of the Torn Page," you had letter clues as well as language and meaning clues. Another word for letter clues is <u>graphic clues</u>. Sometimes the letters remind us of how the words sound when we say them out loud. These are also called <u>phonics clues</u>.

Pictures and symbols are also <u>graphic clues</u>. For example, the lines under the words <u>graphic clues</u> tell you that those words are important.

This poem also had <u>rhyming clues</u>, clues also based on sound and rhythms. Michele and Jacob disagreed about whether all these clues made the case easier.

## Conversation

JACOB: The letter clues made it easier to solve the case. When I saw the letter *n*, I knew that word must be *nest*, especially since *nest* rhymes with *best*.

MICHELE: Yes, but sometimes the letters made it harder. I thought it should say, "Let's hide in the leaves." But that word was supposed to start with *s*.

JACOB: Yeah, you're right. And the word with the *s* was supposed to rhyme with *afraid*.

MICHELE: Well, "Let's hide in the leaves" makes sense, so I just ignored the *s*.

JACOB: I decided on "Let's hide in the stream," but it bothers me that it doesn't rhyme with *afraid*. And I'm not sure squirrels would hide in a stream.

MICHELE: Well, I'm sticking with *leaves*. All my life when I've come to a word I don't know, I tried to sound it out. But now I think that the meaning is more important than making it sound right. The story has to make sense. When I'm reading and I get stuck, I'll look at the graphic clues, but I'll be thinking, "What makes sense?"

© 1999 by Debra Goodman.
*From* The Reading Detective
Club. *Portsmouth, NH:
Heinemann.*

*Jacob used the graphic clues to help solve the mystery, but Michele found that the letters didn't always help her to understand the poem. Jacob also tried to find rhyming words for each couplet of this poem. Michele decided to find answers that made sense, even if they didn't rhyme or start with the same letters.*

*What did you decide to do?*

_____

_____

_____

_____

_____

_____

_____

_____

_____

_____

_____

## WHAT'S THE BIG IDEA?

**Graphic clues (like letters) and pattern clues (like rhymes) give reading detectives more information. It's up to the reader to decide which clues are important. The most important clues help us make meaning. We use all the clues together to make sense of what we read. <u>The main purpose of reading is making sense.</u>**

*So let's put all your clues and strategies to the test in . . . "The Case of the Gluey Page"!*

© 1999 by Debra Goodman. *From* The Reading Detective Club. *Portsmouth, NH: Heinemann.*

# The Case of the Gluey Page

Jacob was a famous detective. One day, Michele came into Jacob's house. Jacob was watching TV.

"Well," Jacob said when the commercial came on, "what did your brother do this time?"

"This time he got hold of some glue and dumped it on one of my books," Michele said. "The good thing is that it's one of my baby books. I was going to give it to him anyway. But I thought it would be fun to see if you could solve this one."

Jacob looked at the page. He groaned. "Half the words are covered up!" He threw the book on the floor and went back to watching TV.

Michele smiled. "I finally found one you can't solve."

Jacob stood up and grabbed the book. He turned the TV off. "Now you've made me mad," he said. "I'll solve this case if it takes me all day."

**DETECTIVES: Write the missing words in the space below.**

Four little monkeys jumping on the bed.
One fell off and bumped his head.
Mama called the doctor and the doctor said,
"No more monkeys jumping on the bed."

Three little monkeys jumping o
One fell off and bumped
Mama called the
"No more m

Two litt
One fell o
Mama calle
"No more mon

One little monk
One fell off and b
Mama called the do
"That's what you get

# DEBRIEFING:
# The Case of the Gluey Page

## *Conversation*

JACOB: Hey, that was easy. It had the most missing words, but it was as easy as "The Case of the Missing Word."

MICHELE: That's because we already knew that little rhyme.

JACOB: No, I had never heard it before.

MICHELE: I can't believe that!

JACOB: It's true. Once you read the first verse, you know the whole thing. Except for the very last line.

MICHELE: Yeah. It's pretty predictable. I guess if something is predictable, it's easier to read.

JACOB: I think reading detectives are story detectives. When you read "Once upon a ____," you know the next word has to be *time*. I'd call that a *story clue*.

MICHELE: Yeah. And the strategy is to make a prediction. It's when you look at the whole story that you can tell what the big ideas are. Like when you thought it would say, "The pigs went out . . ."

JACOB: And that's why sometimes you have to read the whole story to figure out missing words. You know, reading is probably the best way to figure out what words mean, too. You get the meaning from the story.

MICHELE: I'm still mad at my brother, but it's sort of fun to figure out missing words and smudged words. From now on, when I'm reading a book and I come to a word I don't know, I think I'll just say "smudge" and keep reading.

JACOB: That's a good idea. And if the word is important in the story, you can probably figure out what it means while you're reading.

MICHELE: You know, every story is like a mystery—and every reader is like a reading detective. Hey, let's start a Reading Detective Club.

JACOB: Great idea, even if I didn't think of it myself. The reading detective business is fun. Let's make a list of reading strategies for our club.

*© 1999 by Debra Goodman. From* The Reading Detective Club. *Portsmouth, NH: Heinemann.*

## Strategies for Reading Detectives

*(You can add to this list as you go on.)*

WHEN I'M READING, AND I COME TO SOMETHING CONFUSING:

*I ask myself, "What makes sense?" (Jacob)*

*I might skip the word if it's not important to the story. (Michele)*

*I reread the last section to try to build up meaning. (Jacob)*

*I read ahead to get more information. (Michele)*

# 2

## *Let's Take a Guess!*

# The Case of the Goldfish

*PSSSST!*

Hi, my name is Scott. I'm six years old.

I have a big sister named Michele. Don't tell her, but I really like her. She hates me. She never plays with me. So I like to get on her nerves. Then she yells at me and has a fit. You should see her!

Michele is really a good reader. Do you think she ever helps me? *No!* She won't even let me touch her books. She gets *very upset* if my hands are a little messy or something.

First grade is a lot of fun. Our teacher, Miss Milz, reads to us all the time. She has hundreds of books. She never yells when we touch them. She even lets us take them home.

I like reading. But sometimes it's hard! Miss Milz says it's okay for us to make mistakes when we read. After all, we're only six years old! She says even grown-ups don't know everything. Our class even wrote a story about it. I hope you like it.

Uh oh! Here comes Michele and her friend Jacob.

MICHELE: *Wait!* We want to read this story too.

SCOTT: No, this is my story. You never let me read your books.

JACOB: If you let us read it, you can join The Reading Detective Club.

SCOTT: Well, okay. Then let's call this "The Case of the Goldfish." Can you guess what it's about?

JACOB: I don't really like guessing. Let's just read the story.

MICHELE: What do you mean? Detectives make guesses all the time.

JACOB: My teacher told me I was being lazy when I was making guesses. She said I wasn't really thinking.

SCOTT: Guessing is thinking. If I get stuck when I read, Miss Milz tells me to take a guess. Then I really have to think.

MICHELE. It's just like when we estimate in math, Jacob. It's like making a prediction.

© 1999 by Debra Goodman. *From* The Reading Detective Club. *Portsmouth, NH: Heinemann.*

JACOB: I like the sound of estimating or predicting better than just guessing.

MICHELE: Pretend the title is a clue, and make a prediction about what will happen. I think it's going to be about some missing goldfish. Scott will probably be the big hero and find them.

JACOB: I predict that the classroom goldfish will get sick and the kids will have to figure out what the problem is.

## The Case of the Goldfish

*What do you guess the story will be about?*

My prediction:

_____

_____

_____

_____

_____

_____

_____

*Share your predictions with your friends.*

_____

My friends' predictions:

_____

_____

_____

_____

_____

# The Case of the Goldfish, Part 1

**WARNING**

**Don't read out of order. Go back to page 81.**

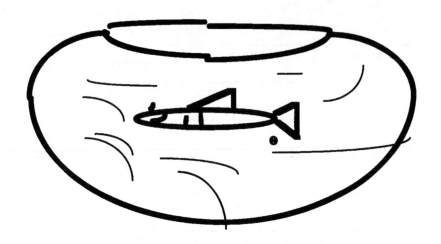

Spring vacation was over and Scott couldn't wait to get to school. He wanted to show Miss Milz a story he had written at home. It was called, "How Scott Drove His Sister Crazy."

Scott arrived at Way School before the school buses, and he ran to his classroom. But when he got to Room 14, no one was there—not even Miss Milz. Scott walked over to the mailboxes to write a note to Miss Milz.

There was a big fishbowl on the table. Scott had never seen it before. A bright, orange goldfish was swimming in the bowl. Scott watched it swimming around and around, opening and closing its mouth.

Then Scott saw a box of fish food next to the bowl. A note was taped to the box. Scott read the note:

Please take care of my fish. Her name is Mergatroyd.

© 1999 by Debra Goodman. From The Reading Detective Club. Portsmouth, NH: Heinemann.

"Her name is *what?!*" Scott said.

Just then all the kids started coming into Room 14.

"Look!" Scott shouted. "Somebody left us a goldfish."

"Who left it here?" Vicki asked. "Can we keep it?"

Scott said, "They left a note, but they didn't sign it. I can't read the fish's name."

Vicki read the note. "Her name is *what?*"

"Let me see it," Todd said. Todd was a very good reader. "'Please take care of my fish,'" he read. "'Her name is . . .' *what?*"

"That's what I said," said Scott.

The children passed the note around, but no one could read the fish's name. Even Caroline couldn't figure it out. "Her name is Mercury? No, that isn't right."

**WARNING**

**Don't read out of order. Go back to page 81.**

© *1999 by Debra Goodman.*
*From* The Reading Detective
Club. *Portsmouth, NH:*
*Heinemann.*

## Conversation

MICHELE: Well, the story wasn't about a missing goldfish. I was wrong about that. But I was right about Scott being the big hero.

JACOB: My prediction about the fish being sick was wrong, too. But I knew that as soon as I read half the page. Especially the note.

SCOTT: Miss Milz says guesses aren't right or wrong. First you make a guess, then you keep reading for more information.

MICHELE: Scott's right. Just because the story is different than we expected doesn't mean we didn't make good guesses. After all, the only clue we had to go on was the title.

JACOB: Yeah. I don't know why my teacher said guessing means you're not thinking. We both made good guesses. We *were* thinking.

SCOTT: So now that you have more clues, can you guess what the story's about?

JACOB: Before we guess, let's list the clues we've read so far.

## Clues for The Case of the Goldfish

*Well, we know it's about a goldfish left in Room 14. (Scott)*

*It says, "Scott had never seen it before." (Michele)*

*There's a note on the fish food, so it's not Miss Milz' fish. (Jacob)*

*Detectives: What other clues did you notice?*

_____

_____

_____

_____

_____

_____

© 1999 by Debra Goodman. *From* The Reading Detective Club. *Portsmouth, NH: Heinemann.*

DETECTIVES: *Now that you've made a list of clues, where do you think the fish came from? What do you think the children will decide to do about her name?*

_____

_____

_____

_____

_____

_____

*P. S. You can keep adding to your list of clues as you read the next pages.*

MORE CLUES:
_____

_____

_____

_____

_____

_____

_____

_____

# The Case of the Goldfish, Part 2

**WARNING**

**Don't read out of order. Go back to page 81.**

Tagg said, "Let's just call her Mary. She won't know the difference."

Scott shook his head. "That's not her right name."

In a little while, Miss Milz came in with some books from the media center. All the kids started shouting. "Look. Someone left us a fish to take care of."

Scott grabbed his teacher's hand and pulled her over to the desk. "I found it here this morning," he said. "Is this some kind of joke?"

Miss Milz was just as surprised as the children. She picked up the goldfish bowl and put it on a table where all the children could see it.

"What a pretty goldfish," she said. "I wonder who left it here."

"There's a note," Vicki said. "We all read it, but we don't know how to say the name."

Miss Milz copied the note onto the blackboard:

> *Please take care of my fish.*
> *Her name is Mergatroyd.*

Everyone read the message again. "How do you say the fish's name?" Caroline asked.

"I don't know," said Miss Milz. "I've never seen that name before."

"Well, if Miss Milz doesn't know, then nobody knows," said Todd.

"Somebody knows," Scott insisted. "Somebody left that fish here."

"Well, we don't know," Tagg said. "I still say, let's call her Mary."

"I think that's a good idea," Miss Milz said.

So the kids called the goldfish "Mary." They took turns feeding her every day, and they added fresh water to her bowl once a week. All the children liked to watch Mary swim around in her bowl, opening and closing her mouth.

© 1999 by Debra Goodman.
*From* The Reading Detective
Club. Portsmouth, NH:
*Heinemann.*

Miss Milz put some paper and pencils next to the bowl and encouraged the children to draw and write the things they noticed about Mary. The children read books and learned about Mary's gills and fins and scales.

After a while they forgot all about the note.

**WARNING**

**Don't read out of order. Go back to page 81.**

## Conversation

JACOB: Is that the end of the story? It doesn't seem like such a great ending. They never found out who brought the fish to the school.

SCOTT: No. There's one more page.

MICHELE: I didn't think that could be the ending, either.

SCOTT: How do you think the story ends?

MICHELE: Well, Scott. Since you're the big hero, I think you should solve the story. Maybe you take the note and look for someone with matching handwriting.

JACOB: No. I think the person who left the fish is in the hospital dying of cancer or something like that.


DETECTIVES: *How would you end the story? Will the children ever find out who brought the fish? Will they learn to say the fish's name? Write your own ending before you read the rest of the story.*

_____

_____

_____

_____

_____

_____

_____

_____

© *1999 by Debra Goodman. From* The Reading Detective Club. *Portsmouth, NH: Heinemann.*

# The Case of the Goldfish, Part 3

**WARNING**

**Don't read out of order. Go back to page 81.**

One day Joe came to visit Room 14. He was the school custodian. He kept the school clean and fixed things when they were broken. The children liked Joe. Joe walked over to the goldfish table, where Scott and Vicki were drawing a picture of Mary with markers.

"How's Mergatroyd?" Joe asked. "Are you taking good care of my little fish?"

"*What?*" Vicki shouted. She laughed at the funny-sounding word.

"Mergatroyd. My fish," Joe said. He pointed to the fishbowl on the table. "There she is. Mergatroyd! You're looking just great!"

"That's *your* fish?" Scott asked. "We didn't know whose fish it was. We didn't know how to say her name."

"Even Miss Milz didn't know," said Vicki.

Joe burst out laughing. All the children looked up from their work. "I must have forgotten to sign my name to that note," he said. "But how do you like Mergatroyd?"

"We like her," Caroline said. "But do you mind if we call her Mary?"

Joe shrugged his shoulders. "Okay with me," he said. "She doesn't care what you call her as long as she gets fed. I got too busy to take care of her, and I thought you girls and boys would like to help."

The children in Room 14 took care of Mergatroyd for the rest of the year. But they always called her "Mary."

© 1999 by Debra Goodman. *From* The Reading Detective Club. *Portsmouth, NH: Heinemann.*

# DEBRIEFING:
# The Case of the Goldfish

## *Conversation*

MICHELE: I liked my ending better than that one. The kids didn't really solve the mystery in the story ending. The mystery just solved itself.

SCOTT: Yeah, but it fooled you, didn't it? Nothing like a good surprise.

JACOB: But we still don't know how to pronounce that name. I hate that!!

SCOTT: Well, actually, all the first-grade authors learned how to say it when we were writing this story. We wanted to think of a name that would be hard to say. Joe came in while we were writing the story, and he suggested that name.

MICHELE: You *know* how to say it! You've known all along. Well, say it! Come on—out with it!

SCOTT: NO! Miss Milz said not to tell anyone unless you get The Big Idea.

### WHAT'S THE BIG IDEA?

MICHELE: Well, I think The Big Idea is that if you're reading a name and you don't know how to pronounce it, it's okay to use another name instead.

JACOB: Yeah. The important meaning of the note was: *Take care of my fish.* By the time they figured out how to say her name, the fish could have died.

SCOTT: You're both right. Miss Milz says there are no wrong answers. My Big Idea is that even grown-ups don't know everything.

DETECTIVES: *What do you think is The Big Idea?*

_____

_____

_____

_____

*© 1999 by Debra Goodman. From* The Reading Detective Club. *Portsmouth, NH: Heinemann.*

## Conversation

MICHELE: Okay, smarty-pants. Tell us the fish's name. You know, it's okay to call a fish Mary in a story. But I wouldn't want to be called Mary just because someone couldn't say Michele.

SCOTT: Miss Milz told us that too. One of the kids is named Franamina, and we wanted to call her Fran, but Miss Milz says that's not nice if it's a real person and not a story.

JACOB: Okay already. How do you say it?

SCOTT: Mergatroyd. Joe told us how to write it so you can read it and say it. *Mer-* like in *mermaid, ga-* like "I'm *ga-na* get you," and *troyd* rhymes with *droid* or *annoyed.* Mergatroyd.

JACOB: Mer- ga- troyd. I can't help it. I like to *know* things.

MICHELE: It's fun to know things, but guessing was fun, too. I think making predictions is a good reading strategy. Remember when we read "The Case of the Gluey Page"? You thought it was easy because it was predictable.

JACOB. Yeah. I guess we always make predictions when we read. It probably helps us understand the story better.

MICHELE: It probably helps to read faster, too. You're kind of thinking ahead of where you're reading.

SCOTT: You guys are thinking way ahead of me. I just know that guessing makes stories more interesting.

JACOB: Sure. Like you can't wait to see what happens. And all my life I thought guessing was bad!

MICHELE: Well, if you take a guess and keep reading, the story helps you find out if you had the right idea. If your guess doesn't make sense, then you stop and figure out what went wrong.

SCOTT: Yeah, and there aren't really right answers since you're just taking a guess. You don't really know for sure what the author will do next.

MICHELE: You mean there aren't really any "wrong answers"—since all predictions are "right" until you get more information.

JACOB: So making a mistake is not a big deal, is it? In fact, it seems like mistakes are an important part of reading!

© 1999 by Debra Goodman.
*From* The Reading Detective
Club. *Portsmouth, NH:
Heinemann.*

# 2
## *Everybody Makes Mistakes*

OOPS!

Did I write "Part Two"?
I meant to write "Part Thee."
Did I write "Thee"?
I meant to rite "Three."

Did I write "rite"?
Well, I didn't write right—
did I?

I'll just write,
"The And."

Oops, I mean . . .
The End.

(See what I mean?)


*And now . . .*
*"The Case of the Missing Mom"*

# The Case of the Missing Mom

Jacob was a famous detective. One day, as he was sorting through his magic cards, Michele came into his "office." Jacob was sitting on his bed.

Michele said, "I think we should be partners."

Jacob said, "I don't think so. I like to work alone."

Michele sat down in an old armchair. "What case are you working on now?" she asked.

Jacob didn't say anything for a while. Then he walked over to the door. "Right now I'm solving the case of the kid listening at the door," he said.

Jacob pulled the door open. Scott fell into the room. "I want to be a partner too," he said.

"Why should we make you a partner?" asked Michele. "You're just a little kid."

"Who says I'm making *anybody* my partner?" said Jacob.

Scott waved a piece of paper in the air. "You should make me your partner because I've got another mystery for us to solve."

"Let's see that," said Jacob.

"Not unless we're partners," said Scott.

"You can be my assistant," said Jacob.

Michele jumped up and started yelling. "Hey, what about me?"

"You don't have any cases to solve, do you?" said Jacob.

Scott said, "Jacob, you can't see the case unless we're *all* partners. You and me *and* Michele."

"Hey, thanks, Scott," Michele said.

Scott smiled.

Jacob frowned. "Okay, it's a deal. Let's see the case."

Scott put the story down on Jacob's desk where they could all read it together. "My mom gave this to me," he said. "She said it's about a man who thinks kids aren't important."

"We'll see about that," said Michele.

© 1999 by Debra Goodman. From The Reading Detective Club. Portsmouth, NH: Heinemann.

## IS YOUR MOM AT HOME?
Retold by Debi Goodman

One summer day a boy sat on the front steps of a large house. The day was hot and sunny, and the boy was licking a triple-scoop ice cream cone.

A man came walking up to the house. He asked, "Little boy, is your mother at home?"

The boy looked up at the man. "Hi," said the bay, "What's your name? I've got a triple-scoop ice cream cone!"

"I don't not have time to talk to little boys," the man said. "Is your mother at home or not?"

"Yes," said the boy, "My mom is at home."

So the man walked up the steps to the porch. He knacked on the door. Nobody answered the door. He knocked a little harder. Nobody answered the dore.

The man looked back at the boy. The boy sat licking his ice creem cone. The man said, "Little boy, are you sure your mother is home?"

"Yes, I'm sure," the boy sad.

The man pounded on the door with his fist. Nobody answered the door. The man looked at the the boy again. His face was red with anger. "Little boy," he shouted. "I thought you said your mother was home."

"My mother is hume," said the boy.

"Well, why doesn't she she answer the door?" The man shouted even louder.

"Because," said boy. "My mom *is* at home. But this is *not* my house."

© 1999 by Debra Goodman. From The Reading Detective Club. Portsmouth, NH: Heinemann.

# DEBRIEFING:
# The Case of the Missing Mom

*Well, how'd you like my story? It's actually an old joke I heard when I was little. Have you ever seen a book that was retold by the author? Anyone can retell a folktale or an old story. You should try it. Just be careful not to retell an original story written by another author.*

## Conversation

SCOTT: That was pretty funny. I liked that case, didn't you?

JACOB: I don't get it. I mean, I get the joke, but what's the mystery? We know where the boy's mom is. And those mistakes got on my nerves.

SCOTT: What mistakes?

MICHELE: I liked the story, but I noticed some mistakes too.

SCOTT: *What* mistakes??

JACOB: Well, for one thing, *cream* is spelled wrong in *ice cream.*

MICHELE: I didn't notice that one, but I saw some others. Maybe that's the mystery—to find all the mistakes.

JACOB: Okay, let's get paper and pencils and see who can find the most mistakes.

SCOTT: *What mistakes!!??*

DETECTIVES: *Did you notice any mistakes in the story? Scott read the whole story, and he got the joke, but he didn't notice any mistakes. Actually, there are* ten *mistakes in the story "Is Your Mom at Home?" How many can you find?*

© 1999 by Debra Goodman. *From* The Reading Detective Club. *Portsmouth, NH: Heinemann.*

*Here's a chart for listing all the mistakes:*

1. *The word* ice cream *is spelled* ice creem *near the end.*
_____

2. _____

3. _____

4. _____

5. _____

6. _____

7. _____

8. _____

9. _____

10. _____

*Did you find all ten mistakes? You might want to compare your answer with the other detective clubs in your class. Why do you think you didn't notice all of the mistakes the first time you read the story?*

*Just for fun, give the story to a grown-up to read. <u>Don't tell the grown-ups that there are mistakes in the story</u>. See if they even notice. If they do, see if they can find the ten mistakes.*

## Everybody Makes Mistakes
## Conversation

JACOB: That was really hard. I noticed some mistakes the first time I read the story, but I didn't notice all ten.

SCOTT: I didn't notice any. I thought it was just a funny story.

MICHELE: I wonder why we didn't notice all of the mistakes. They seem so obvious once you do find them.

JACOB: Hmm. You know, this just proves that we pay attention to meaning clues first. If the story is making sense, we just keep reading and we don't even look at all the letters.

MICHELE: We don't even look at all the words. How can you not see a whole word?

SCOTT: Hey! I bet it's because we're predicting again. But I can't really explain it.

MICHELE: I think you're right. We're predicting what we're about to read. We see what we *think* we'll see. If it makes sense, we just keep going. That's amazing!

JACOB: We must correct the printed mistakes in our head without even knowing it! Our brain doesn't expect the mistakes so we don't see them.

MICHELE: Do we correct them, or do we not even notice them? Maybe we just make up the whole story as we go along.

JACOB: This is too deep for me.

SCOTT: I'm glad you said that 'cause you lost me a long time ago.

DETECTIVES: *Why do you think readers don't notice the mistakes in the story? You can write down your thoughts here.*

**WHAT'S THE BIG IDEA?**

_____

_____

_____

_____

© 1999 by Debra Goodman.
From The Reading Detective
Club. Portsmouth, NH:
Heinemann.

## Conversation

JACOB: I always think it's my fault if I have a problem reading something. Maybe it's the author's fault. Maybe the author didn't do a good job of writing.

MICHELE: Or maybe it's just a typo and the proofreader didn't notice it.

SCOTT: Hey, I must be a really good reader if I can fix the author's mistakes without even knowing it.

MICHELE: You just might be right. It's amazing to know that even editors who have a job of checking for mistakes don't always notice all the mistakes.

SCOTT: Like Miss Milz says, everybody makes mistakes, even grown-ups.

MICHELE: I liked "The Case of the Missing Mom." It was fun looking for all the mistakes. I bet I can write a story and hide mistakes like that.

JACOB: You're on. I'll write a story, too.

SCOTT: Me too!

JACOB: We'll each put in five mistakes so we can time how long it takes the others to find them.

MICHELE: Let's see who does the best job at hiding their mistakes.

## WHAT'S THE BIG IDEA?

No one can read or write without making mistakes. Our minds are busy predicting and making sense of the story. Sometimes we "fix" the author's mistakes. Sometimes we understand the story differently from the author's story. This is because as readers we create our own story when we read. Making mistakes is part of reading and writing.

© 1999 by Debra Goodman. From The Reading Detective Club. Portsmouth, NH: Heinemann.

# The Case of the Damaged Books

by Michele

Michele was a famouse detective. But she also loved to read books. She kept all of her books in her bookshelves near her bed. She even alphabetized them by the title. That way, she could always find her favorite books and read them again and agin.

One day Michele noticed a book in the wrong place. When she she looked at it, she saw it was damaged. Words were crossed out! Another day, she noticed a book under her bed. Messy fingerprints had smudged up her nice storys! The next day she found the culprit. Her brother Scott was sitting on her bed reading a book of poems. When she tried to grab her book, the page got torn!

This was the last straw, Michele thought. Scott was really in for it now. But, in the meantime, Michele had taken each book to her friend Jacob. Together they could read each book. It was so much fun that Michele actually folded and glued the page of one of her boks so they would have more mysteries to solve.

Michele decided to start the Reeding Detective Club. Jacob and Scott immediately wanted to join up!

© 1999 by Debra Goodman. From The Reading Detective Club. Portsmouth, NH: Heinemann.

JACOB: Hey, that was too easy. They were all spelling mistakes.

MICHELE: No, they weren't. Hey, why did you put down *famouse*?

JACOB: 'Cause it's not supposed to have an *e* at the end.

MICHELE: Oops. I guess there are six mistakes.

SCOTT: Don't worry—everyone makes mistakes.

JACOB: Your story makes it look like you're the great detective. I suspected that you glued that page down. And you made me think Scott did it.

SCOTT: Yeah. You blame me for everything.

MICHELE: It's just a story. It's fiction, you know. Not necessarily true.

SCOTT AND JACOB: Oh sure!


DETECTIVES: *Can you find six mistakes?*

1. _____

2. _____

3. _____

4. _____

5. _____

6. _____

# The Case of the Smashed Chicken

by Jacob

Jacob was a famous detective. He had solved many brilliant cases. He even had two sidekicks, Michele and Scott. Jacob was also a grate reader. He had started a Reading Detective Club.

One day, when Jacob was reading, she came across this question:

*"Why did the chicken cross the road?"*

"Look," Jacob said to Michele and Scott. "A new mystery for us to solve. *Why did the chicken cross the road?*"

"That's easy," Scott sade, "to get to the other side."

"Too obvious," said Jacob.

"To get away from the fox?" Scott said.

"Too stoopid," said Jacob. "But either way, a truck coming and and he's one smashed chicken."

Scott laughed.

"You're both crazy," said Michele, who trying to read. "Laughing at smashed chickens! Besides, that's not a mystery. It's an old joke."

"I suppose your right," Jacob said. "But he's still one dead chicken."

© 1999 by Debra Goodman.
From The Reading Detective
Club. Portsmouth, NH:
Heinemann.

SCOTT: That cracked me up!

MICHELE: Sidekicks. What do you mean, sidekicks???

JACOB: Just fiction, you know.

MICHELE: Well, anyway, I found all eight mistakes. And you left the same word out twice.

JACOB: I didn't leave out any words. And there are only six mistakes. Oh . . . I was typing so fast on the computer, I guess I did leave some words out.

DETECTIVES: *Did you find all eight mistakes?*

1. _____

2. _____

3. _____

4. _____

5. _____

6. _____

7. _____

8. _____

© 1999 by Debra Goodman.
From The Reading Detective
Club. Portsmouth, NH:
Heinemann.

# The Kas of the Stoopid Chekin

by Scott

Wan day thar wuz a chekin. Her name wuz Michele.
Michele kapt heren all thes joks abot a chekin krasing the
rod. He waned to be famus lik the chekin in all the joks. So
he desidid to kras the rod. All the othr chekinz wornd hem
not to leev the frm. Its danjerus out thar, tha sed. You kood
get last. You kood get hit by a truk. You kood get keld.

     Michele woden lesin to the othr chekinz. I'm goen to be
famus, she thot. He iknord all the wornens. He desidid to
lev that day. So he wakt out of the gat and then she lef the
frm and went akras the rod. And tha navr saw her agin.

MICHELE AND JACOB: *What?!*

SCOTT: What's wrong?

JACOB: You were only supposed to put in five mistakes. I can't even
    read this. Every word is spelled wrong.

SCOTT: What did you expect? I'm just six years old. In our class, we
    spell the best we can. Miss Milz says that's how we learn to write.

MICHELE: Oh yeah, I heard about this at Open House. It's called
    *invented spelling.* This way, kids can write stories even when they
    don't know how to spell a lot of words.

JACOB: Now that I look at it again, not all of the words are spelled
    wrong. There's *the, and, of, you, out, saw* . . .

MICHELE: Yeah. Actually, it's not bad for a six-year-old.

SCOTT: Hey, thanks!

MICHELE: I think I can read it. You just kind of say the letters the way
    they sound: One day there was a . . .

JACOB: Chicken?

MICHELE: His name was Michele . . . But Scott, why do you write *his*
    for *her* and then *he* for *she?*

SCOTT: Those were the mistakes I put in on purpose.

JACOB: Actually, this may be the best case yet!

© *1999 by Debra Goodman.*
*From* The Reading Detective
Club. *Portsmouth, NH:*
*Heinemann.*

DETECTIVES: *Can you read "The Kas of the Stoopid Chekin?" Write your version here:*

_____

_____

_____

_____

_____

_____

_____

_____

_____

_____

_____

_____

_____

_____

DETECTIVES: *If you thought it was fun reading Scott's story with all of the "invented spellings," you might enjoy Investigation #4 on page 166.*

© *1999 by Debra Goodman. From* The Reading Detective Club. *Portsmouth, NH: Heinemann.*

DETECTIVES: *Now it's your turn! Would you like to write a story with hidden mistakes? Use this page to write your story. Then add some hidden mistakes. See if your club members can find the mistakes. You might want to make copies of your stories and put them in your own detective club book.*

## The Case of _____

by _____

_____

_____

_____

_____

_____

_____

_____

_____

_____

_____

**Mistakes:**

1. _____

2. _____

3. _____

4. _____

5. _____

# The Case of the Great Mistake

*Have you ever noticed mistakes in something you're reading? In these stories the mistakes were made by the authors. Book authors and other writers have editors and proofreaders to read over their text and make corrections. Each book is read many times before it's printed, but it's almost impossible to print a book without any mistakes. You can use this chart to keep track of mistakes that you find in your reading materials.*

## Mistakes We've Noticed in Published Texts

_____

_____

_____

_____

_____

_____

_____

_____

_____

_____

_____

_____

## Exploring Miscues

### Conversation

MICHELE: Hey, I was just thinking that if spelling mistakes are called *invented spelling*, what do reading detectives call reading mistakes?

JACOB: Yeah. Because *mistake* always sounds like you did something wrong. I hate making mistakes.

MICHELE: Well, everyone makes mistakes. But reading mistakes aren't really wrong. Sometimes they help you make sense.

SCOTT: Like when I read "The Case of the Missing Mom" and didn't notice any of the printed mistakes?

JACOB: Yeah. I'm beginning to think mistakes are *okay!*

MICHELE: Anyway, you know how reading detectives make *predictions* when other people might say we're just *guessing*? There must be a better word than *mistake.*

SCOTT: Oh, I know what you mean. When Miss Milz is reading and she makes a mistake, she says, "Look, I made a miscue."

JACOB: A *miscue?*

SCOTT: Yeah. Our class is collecting some funny miscues.

JACOB: Funny miscues?

SCOTT: Yeah, they can be really funny. My friend Carol told us a funny one. She was on a long car ride with her family. They hadn't stopped for a long time and she was getting very hungry. She saw a sign that said "Pizza ahead." So she shouted, "Stop, stop!" Her mom shouted, "What is it?" Carol shouted, "Stop. I want pizza. I saw a sign that said, 'Pizza ahead.'" But when they came to the exit, they didn't see any pizza places. They saw a sign that said, "Peoria, Illinois." Carol and her mom finally figured out that the sign had said, "Peoria ahead."

MICHELE: Well I can see why she would think it said *pizza.* If you're hungry, you're probably looking for some food! You know, predicting is kind of like you start with your own meaning whenever you're reading. And you bring your feelings, too. If you're hungry, you might think you're reading about food. Like wishful thinking.

JACOB: I wonder why Miss Milz calls reading mistakes *miscues?*

SCOTT: She says her friend Dr. Goodman thought of the word *miscue* because mistakes are not really bad. Mistakes can show that you're really thinking.

© 1999 by Debra Goodman. From The Reading Detective Club. Portsmouth, NH: Heinemann.

JACOB: The word *cue* reminds me of the word *clue*. Like, you missed a *clue*.

MICHELE: I just remembered. I was watching a football game and they said the football player "miscued" on the play. He was in the wrong place when they threw the ball. Something like that.

JACOB: So when you "miscue," you are still using the reading clues. You use the clues to make a different prediction than the author or some other readers might.

MICHELE: Yeah! It's not really a mistake because you're still using the clues. You're still trying to figure out what makes sense.

SCOTT: Miss Milz says Dr. Goodman likes to collect miscues. He uses them to learn about how people read. When Miss Milz listens to us read, she likes to collect miscues too.

MICHELE: I bet it's fun to collect reading miscues. Just like we enjoyed looking at Scott's invented spellings.

SCOTT: You guys had invented spellings too!!!

JACOB: Sure. Sure.

SCOTT: I think it would be fun to collect miscues too.

JACOB: Let's ask people if they remember some funny mistakes they made when they read.

## WHAT'S THE BIG IDEA?

All readers (even grown-ups) make miscues when they read. We make miscues because we're busy interpreting the written clues in order to make sense out of what we're reading. Most of the time we don't notice our miscues, because they don't really change the meaning of the text. If the miscue changes the meaning of the written text, we usually notice it. Then we go back and try to correct the miscue.

*© 1999 by Debra Goodman. From* The Reading Detective Club. *Portsmouth, NH: Heinemann.*

## The Funniest Miscues from Our Detective Club

_____

_____

_____

_____

_____

_____

_____

_____

_____

_____

_____

_____

_____

_____

_____

DETECTIVES: *If you enjoyed collecting miscues, try the investigation on page 159 called Studying Our Own Miscues.*

# 4
# *Playing with Language*

# The Case of the Norful Snig

One day Scott was sitting in his room drawing pictures. His sister Michele came into his room and sat down on his bed.

"Hey," Scott said. "No fair coming in without my permission. That's what you always tell me."

"So I'll leave," Michele said without getting up from the bed.

"That's okay," Scott told her. "Want to draw some pictures?"

Michele looked over at Scott's desk. "Where'd you get all that paper?"

"Miss Milz was cleaning out her file cabinet," Scott said. "This is all scrap paper that she didn't need. See, it has writing on one side."

Michele picked up a sheet of paper to start drawing. She looked at the printed side. "What's this??" she said, "It says, 'The Norful Snig' . . . It looks like a story, but it's got a whole lot of words I don't know."

"It has words *you* don't know?" Scott said. "I thought you knew everything! Let me see."

Michele showed Scott the story.

"This looks like a case for The Reading Detective Club," Scott said.

They ran to show the story to Jacob.

Jacob took a look at the story. At the end of the story, there were some questions. "This doesn't make any sense," said Jacob. "But I think I can answer the questions."

*© 1999 by Debra Goodman. From* The Reading Detective Club. *Portsmouth, NH: Heinemann.*

## THE NORFUL SNIG

Moffy and Targy were best bops. They velled the same borgs. The vorgled the same bagids. They hek all the same bops. Every bewt they rogged to prock together. Every zewt they rogged moom together. On Governog they velled together all nog.

One nog a norful snig borved onto the grog. Moffy vorgled the norful snig. But Targy did weerk vorgle the norful snig one bit. Targy rassed, "That norful snig is a quaz! That snig is the boofiest quaz I've every progged! I'm weerk velling with a boofy snig like that."

Moffy rassed, "You're just crigging zaz. Your the zazest quaz here. You yook what you bov. I'm burging to vell with my norful bop."

"And I'm burging moom!" grazzed Targy.

All nog Moffy velled with the norful snig. All nog Targy regged moom. Flomily Targy rassed, "There's briggle to yook without Moffy. I've never had such a zoggy nog. It's weerk any grezle without Moffy."

So Targy burged to Moffy's moot. Moffy and the norful snig were velling belthorgen.

"Can I vell?" tassed Targy.

Moffy tragged at Targy. "Come on," he rassed.

"You're it," rassed the norful snig.

Now Moffy and Targy had a norful bop.

© 1999 by Debra Goodman. *From* The Reading Detective Club. *Portsmouth, NH: Heinemann.*

## Comprehension Questions

1. Who was Targy's best bop?
   A. Moffy
   B. Taffy
   C. Laffy
   D. Daffy

2. Why borved onto the grog?
   A. a norful snig
   B. a belthorgen
   C. a boofy quaz
   D. a best bop

3. What did Targy grazz to Moffy?
   A. I'm burging nowhere.
   B. I'm burging moom.
   C. I'm velling belthorgen.
   D. I'm a boofy quaz.

4. Who vorgled the norful snig?
   A. Targy
   B. Moffy
   C. Margy
   D. Taffy

5. What were Moffy and the norful snig velling?
   A. brickabracka
   B. four square
   C. I'm not telling
   D. belthorgen

6. What is the main idea of this story?
   A. Moffy and Targy were best bops.
   B. Moffy and Targy had a norful bop.
   C. Moffy and Targy were boofy snigs.
   D. The norful snig was a quaz.

© 1999 by Debra Goodman.
From The Reading Detective
Club. Portsmouth, NH:
Heinemann.

# DEBRIEFING:
# The Case of the Norful Snig

DETECTIVES: *Did you get the "right" answer to all of the "comprehension questions"? What were the clues in this story that helped you answer the questions?*

**Question**

1. Who was Targy's best bop?

**Clues**

The story said, "Moffy and Targy were best bops," so the answer had to be "Moffy."

2. Who borved onto the grog?

3. What did Targy grazz to Moffy?

4. Who vorgled the norful snig?

5. What were Moffy and the norful snig velling?

6. What is the main idea of this story?

DETECTIVES: *Why do you think you can answer the questions without understanding the story? Talk with your friends. You can write down your thoughts here.*

**WHAT'S THE BIG IDEA?**

_____

_____

_____

_____

© 1999 by Debra Goodman.
*From* The Reading Detective Club. *Portsmouth, NH: Heinemann.*

## Conversation

SCOTT: How come we could get the answers with all those made-up words?

MICHELE: Well, I think we used language clues, like when we solved "The Case of the Messy Hands." It's like the questions *almost* sound like English.

JACOB: Yeah, you're right. You turn the question around and it becomes a sentence in the story.

MICHELE: And the words seem like real words. Like *borved* and *rassed* have an *ed* like past-tense verbs.

SCOTT: Past-tense verbs?

MICHELE: Well, a verb is something you do, like *walk, talk,* and so on. And when you already did something, you say *walked, talked.* You add an *ed* when you spell it. And some of these words have *ed* endings.

JACOB: You're right. And the punctuation gives us clues too. Like there's quotation marks after it says "Moffy rassed."

SCOTT: *Rassed* must mean *said.* Hey, let me look at that.

MICHELE: You know, this reminds me of taking a reading test. They have all those questions at the end of the story. Sometimes I don't understand everything I read, but I can get the right answer anyway.

JACOB: Hey, maybe I should try that. When I don't understand something on a test, I stop and try to figure it out. Then I kind of freeze up—and I get worried and feel so nervous I can hardly take the test . . . that must be why I don't do so well on reading tests.

MICHELE: You don't?

JACOB: No. But from now on I'll just be a detective and keep on reading.

MICHELE: Well, I think reading tests are silly. We don't even understand the story and we can still answer the questions.

SCOTT: Wait a minute. I think I kind of understand this story. Look. This word *bop* is in here a lot. Maybe *bops* means *friends.* Moffy and Targy were best friends . . .

JACOB: Hey, he's right again. Leave it to Scott to always focus on the meaning. Let's see if we can make sense of this story.

© 1999 by Debra Goodman. *From* The Reading Detective Club. *Portsmouth, NH: Heinemann.*

DETECTIVES: *Want to try "translating" "The Case of the Norful Snig"?*
*Below I wrote the story again with spaces between the lines. Can you come*
*up with a story that makes sense?*
    *By the way, you may not come up with the same story as other*
*detective clubs. In fact, your stories might be very different! But the idea is*
*to make up a story that makes sense. (I'm sure you know that by now!) Use*
*a pencil in case you change your mind.*

## *The Norful Snig*

Moffy and Targy were best bops. They velled the same

borgs. The vorgled the same bagids. They hek all the same

bops. Every bewt they rogged to prock together. Every zewt

they rogged moom together. On Governog they velled

together all nog.

One nog a norful snig borved onto the grog. Moffy

vorgled the norful snig. But Targy did weerk vorgle the

norful snig one bit. Targy rassed, "That norful snig is a quaz!

That snig is the boofiest quaz I've every progged! I'm weerk

velling with a boofy snig like that."

Moffy rassed, "You're just crigging zaz. Your the zazest

quaz here. You yook what you bov. I'm burging to vell with

my norful bop."

*© 1999 by Debra Goodman.*
*From* The Reading Detective
Club. *Portsmouth, NH:*
*Heinemann.*

"And I'm burging moom!" grazzed Targy.

All nog Moffy velled with the norful snig. All nog Targy regged moom. Flomily Targy rassed, "There's briggle to yook without Moffy. I've never had such a zoggy nog. It's weerk any grezle without Moffy."

So Targy burged to Moffy's moot. Moffy and the norful snig were velling belthorgen.

"Can I vell?" tassed Targy.

Moffy tragged at Targy. "Come on," he rassed.

"You're it," rassed the norful snig.

Now Moffy and Targy had a norful bop.

HINT: *These words appear more than once:* bop (bops), vell (velled, velling), vorgle (vorgled), hek, rogged, nog, norful, snig, quaz, boofy (boofiest) weerk, moom, yook, rassed, zaz (zazest).

© 1999 by Debra Goodman. From The Reading Detective Club. *Portsmouth, NH: Heinemann.*

# DEBRIEFING:
# The Case of the Norful Snig

## *Conversation*

JACOB: Hey, you know how we found all of those adjectives when we were working on the smudge: "the (smudge) pigs"? I think I can tell where adjectives are in this story, too. Like "the norful snig," sounds like "the little pigs." The "snig" is a thing, like pigs, and "norful" is a describing word.

MICHELE: Yeah, and you found the noun, too. Here it says "the grog," and here it says "the same bagids." I think *the* always comes before a noun.

JACOB: Or if there are two words after *the,* then one is an adjective, like "the norful snig." The order of the words is another kind of language clue.

SCOTT: But here it says "a norful snig," and here it says "a quaz."

JACOB: Good thinking, Scott. I guess *a* or *the* are both clues that say "look for a noun."

SCOTT: What's a noun?

MICHELE: A noun is a thing. Or it could be a person or a place.

JACOB: But words like *idea* and *thought* are nouns, too. You can have "a thought."

SCOTT: Amazing! I never heard of a noun before, but I knew "snig" and "quaz."

MICHELE: That is pretty incredible. Your mind must know what a noun is, even if you don't know the word *noun.*

JACOB: How can that be possible? That doesn't seem right.

MICHELE: I know. But isn't there a difference between *knowing* about something and *talking* about it? When Scott was a baby, he knew how to walk and run and eat and all those things before he knew any words to describe it at all.

SCOTT: I think I see what you mean. We know how to speak our language even if we can't explain it to someone else.

MICHELE: Exactly! Language sure is complicated. But fun, too.

JACOB: You can say that again!

**WHAT'S THE BIG IDEA?**

**We all know the rules of our language, even if we can't explain them. We all use language clues when we read.**

*© 1999 by Debra Goodman. From* The Reading Detective Club. *Portsmouth, NH: Heinemann.*

*When you were reading this story you couldn't use too many meaning clues because almost all of the important ideas in the story, like nouns and verbs, were made-up, nonsense words. But you could answer questions and figure out a story that made sense. This is because the language in the story follows the English language rules, even if the words are made up. Like Scott, you might not be able to describe or explain all of the language clues in the story, but you used them all the same when you were reading and writing your own story.*

## Reading Detectives Use Language Clues

DETECTIVES: *Do you notice any interesting things about language clues in the story, like Michele and Jacob did?*

| Language clues | Examples |
|---|---|
| *Past tense verbs had* ed *at the end. This way we knew they were verbs. (Michele)* | *velled, borved, tassed* |
| *I noticed that quotation marks helped to know which words meant "said" or "asked." (Jacob)* | *"Can I vell?" tassed Targy.* |
| *I noticed that the word* a *means a noun is coming up. And I learned what a noun is! (Scott)* | *That snig is a quaz.* |
| | |
| | |
| | |

© *1999 by Debra Goodman. From* The Reading Detective Club. *Portsmouth, NH: Heinemann.*

# The Shrag of the Glumpy Frinkle

DETECTIVES:
*Michele, Jacob, and Scott thought this was so much fun, they wanted to write their own nonsense story. They thought you might like to read it and see if you can use the language clues to make sense out of it.*

Jissle was a sneemish nudden. One nog Missen slore to Jissle's clibb to veeg Jissle.

"I have a shrag for you," shoffed Missen.

"I can creshen any shrag," Jissle shoffed. "What did your forgle Shoog niss this krimp?"

"That fristy kig gorked my frinkle," Missen sharfled.

Just then Shoog slore into the clibb. "I didn't niss anything," shoffed Shoog. "I've been slimped!"

"Oh yeah," shoffed Missen. "Just tonk at my frinkle!" She yorvled her frinkle to Shoog and Jissle. The frinkle was grook glumpy.

"My frinkle is gorked! Every frik is glumpy! I can't preek my frinkle!" Missen shoffed in a vortle vorg.

"I've never veeged that frinkle in my entire vida," sharfled Shoog. "I've been slimped."

Jissle tonked at Shoog. He tonked at Missen. He tonked at the glumpy, gorked frinkle. "I'm not sure I can creshen this shrag," Jissle shoffed.

Shoog and Missen tonked at Jissle. "You're not a sneemish nodden," they both shoffed. "You're a fristy nodden."

Just then Jissle veeged a snart in the friks of the frinkle. "What's that?" he muffed.

Missen tonked at the snart. It shoffed:

Dear Missen,

I'm very fristy about gorking your frinkle. It was in a biff of your shinkles. When I warsled the shinkles, I warsled the frinkle. Your frinkle got grook glumpy. I hope you have preeked the frinkle already.

Amor, Mom

"Shrag creshened," shoffed Jissle.

HINT!
A "shrag" is a case.

124

DETECTIVES: *Were you able to "preek" "The Shrag of the Glumpy Frinkle"? Want to try writing your own nonsense story? Here are some hints:*

- Write out your story in English (or any language you know well) first, then make up nonsense words for nouns, verbs, adjectives, and adverbs.
- Try to repeat words over and over so your readers can gather more clues to solve the case.
- Make sure you use the same nonsense word for all forms of the English word. For example: say, said, saying = vork, vorked, vorking.
- Good luck!

_____

_____

_____

_____

_____

_____

_____

_____

_____

_____

_____

_____

© *1999 by Debra Goodman.*
*From* The Reading Detective
Club. *Portsmouth, NH:*
*Heinemann.*

# DEBRIEFING:
# The Shrag of the Glumpy Frinkle

## Conversation

SCOTT: It was fun reading and writing nonsense stories. We could even answer questions without understanding the story.

JACOB: Yeah. But pretty soon we wanted to make sense out of the story. I guess when you're reading you always want the text to make sense.

MICHELE: Well, if it doesn't make sense it gets boooorrring pretty fast.

SCOTT: Miss Milz says that if you're reading a book and it doesn't make sense, you should *stop reading*.

JACOB: What a radical idea! But sometimes my teacher makes me read things. What am I supposed to do then?

SCOTT: I don't know. Miss Milz lets us choose our books. If they don't make sense, we stop reading.

JACOB: Well, sometimes you do have to read things, don't you. How about if you're crossing the street, and there's a sign blinking at you. Don't you have to read the sign to know if it says "walk" or "don't walk"?

SCOTT: I never thought of that. You might get in trouble sometimes if you just stop reading. Like if you get a new toy and you can't read the instructions.

JACOB: Yeah. What do you do then?

MICHELE: Use all the clues and strategies you know to try to make sense. And maybe ask a friend to help. All I know is, what's the point in reading if something doesn't make any sense?

SCOTT: Does that mean that meaning clues are more important than language clues or letter clues?

MICHELE: Well, I think so—don't you?

SCOTT: I guess. But if we didn't have language clues, how could we use the meaning clues? Like what if the sentence was backward: "ball kicked boy the."

MICHELE: Yeah. I know the meaning of all those words, but the sentence doesn't make sense.

JACOB: I think the graphic clues are pretty important, too. We wouldn't even have stories if we didn't have letters and punctuation.

**WHAT'S THE BIG IDEA?**

When we read and write, we are trying to *make sense* out of print. Making sense out of print means we use all the clues at the same time. We use meaning clues, language clues, and letter-sound clues.

Linguists (people who study language) talk about three important "language systems": the semantic (meaning) system, the syntactic (language) system, and the graphophonic (letters and sounds) system. The graphophonic system is a combination of graphic clues (written symbols like letters) that we use to read and write and sound clues that we use to talk and listen.

Reading researchers call these three language systems the "cueing systems" that we use when we read. The "cues" that reading researchers are talking about are like the "clues" that reading detectives use. This is why it is called a *miscue* when a reader reads something different from what we might expect.

*In order to make sense out of texts, we need to use all three language systems at the same time. If we only have one or two systems, like the nonsense stories we just read, we can't make any sense out of the text.*

DETECTIVES: *You can use the chart on the next page to write down some examples of reading clues using different language systems. It might be easier to think of examples after you have been reading a book that you've chosen. You might start the chart now and come back to it.*

*I have included an extra box in case you think of another kind of clue system. For example, the "story clues" that we used when we made predictions in "The Case of the Goldfish" could be considered <u>meaning clues</u>, but you might want to call them "story clues." The "rhyming clues" we used in "The Case of the Torn Page" might be considered <u>language clues</u>, but you might want to list them under "pattern clues."*

*© 1999 by Debra Goodman. From* The Reading Detective Club. *Portsmouth, NH: Heinemann.*

# Clues That Reading Detectives Use When They Read

**Meaning Clues:**

_____

_____

_____

_____

_____

_____

_____

**Language Clues:**

_____

_____

_____

_____

_____

_____

_____

_____

**Graphic Clues:**

_____

_____

_____

_____

_____

_____

_____

_____

**Other Clues:**

_____

_____

_____

_____

_____

_____

_____

_____

_____

# 5

# You Are What You Read,
# Or . . . You Read What You Are

The title "You Are What You Read" is a play on words. It's based on the saying "You are what you eat." Have you heard that expression? It means if you eat healthy foods you will be healthy, and if you eat lots of junk food your body might get sick.

But you could also say "You eat what you are." Do you eat grits, cereal, rice, or pancakes for breakfast? Sometimes what you eat depends on where you live. Do you eat arroz con pollo, shwarma, kasha, or hamburgers for dinner? Sometimes what you eat depends on where your family comes from. What do you eat on holidays and special occasions? You might eat many of these foods because you are lucky enough to live near people from many different cultures.

So, "You are what you eat." But also, "You eat what you are."

And "You are what you read," right? Because you learn so much from books. And you can feel so close to your favorite stories and characters.

But did you know that "You read what you are"? The next case will show you what I mean.

Here comes . . . "The Case of the Missing Titles"!

# The Case of the Missing Titles

Jacob was a famous detective. He had solved many important cases.

One day Scott came by with a copy of the school newspaper.

"Look," Scott said. "Some fourth graders wrote articles in the school newspaper. But they left off the titles. The articles don't make any sense."

"What?" said Jacob, "Titles aren't that important. It's probably 'cause you're so little. I bet I can read those articles. Let me see the newspaper."

Jacob read the articles.

"Well?" said Scott.

Jacob shook his head. "I understand all the words," he said, "but these articles don't make any sense at all. I don't think the fourth graders are very good writers."

"I knew you couldn't figure them out," Scott said. "But look at the bottom of the page. The teacher says if you guess the missing titles you can understand the articles."

Jacob looked at the articles again. "It's some kind of trick," he said. "They just don't give you enough information."

Just then Michele walked in. "What's up?" she asked.

Jacob gave her the newspaper to read. She read the articles. "What's the problem?" said Michele.

"You can understand them?" said Jacob.

"They're a little general," Michele said. "But it's easy once you figure out what they're about. Want me to tell you the missing titles?"

"No," Scott and Jacob said at the same time. If Michele could figure out the missing titles, they would too.

*© 1999 by Debra Goodman.*
*From* The Reading Detective
Club. *Portsmouth, NH:*
*Heinemann.*

## School Journal

by Jimmy

This job is important or people could get hurt.

Some people start working while the fall is going on. They say they will have less work to do later. Other people just wait until it's stopped. They say, "Why bother. You'll just have to do it all over again later."

Anyway, everyone comes out after a big fall is over. The idea is to clear everything up so that people can walk safely. It's important to have good equipment. Many people use equipment made out of hard plastic, but other people use metal equipment. Some people get fancy electric equipment, but that can be pretty expensive.

If it's cold and dry, the work is easier. If it's warmer and wet, the heavy stuff makes the job much harder. But one way or another, it's important to get the job done. When everyone in the neighborhood is out working, it can be a lot of fun. After the work is done, everyone can play and build things. Then it's all over until the next big fall.

by LaShanda

Saturday was the best day of my life. I netted the
winning shot on a corner kick. It looped around the
goalie and went right in.

I assisted on our first score, too. I hurled one
toward the center on a throw in, and Tom headed it
into the net. We were tied one to one at the half.

They were good, and we couldn't seem to get off
many shots. They had a lot of tricky plays. Their
defense would pull back and we were called offsides.
But we held strong, too, and kept it to a tie. Finally, I
booted a hard shot at the goal. It bounced off one of
their players behind the net and set up the corner
kick.

The day was ours. I'll remember it the rest of
my life!

Dear Kids:
The fourth graders have been talking about how we
use our past experiences when we read. We've
written some newspaper articles, but we left off the
titles. If you can figure out the missing titles, you
will probably be able to understand the articles.
   Mrs. Nebel

© 1999 by Debra Goodman.
From The Reading Detective
Club. Portsmouth, NH:
Heinemann.

# DEBRIEFING:
# The Case of the Missing Titles

*Detectives: What do you think the articles are about? Can you guess what their titles might be?*

Jimmy's title: _____

Jimmy's article is about:

_____

_____

_____

_____

_____

LaShanda's title: _____

LaShanda's article is about:

_____

_____

_____

_____

_____

DETECTIVES: *Take some time to think, talk, and share your answers with your friends before you read the conversation on the next page.*

© 1999 by Debra Goodman.
From The Reading Detective
Club. Portsmouth, NH:
Heinemann.

# DEBRIEFING: The Case of the Missing Titles—Jimmy's Story

**! WARNING**

Read pages 133–134 before reading this page.

## *Conversation*

JACOB: Jimmy's story is about some kind of job. I guess I would call it "Getting the Job Done." But I still don't get it. What is this job everyone is doing? Jimmy left out too much information.

SCOTT: I would call it "The Big Fall." But what *is* a big fall? At first I thought it was people falling somewhere . . . but that doesn't seem right.

MICHELE: So what else falls? Something that's heavy when it's wet and lighter when it's dry. And you have to clean it up or people will slip and fall . . .

JACOB AND SCOTT: Snow!!

SCOTT: It's a big *snowfall!!*

JACOB: Hey, let me look at it again. Now it all makes sense. You know how some people run out and start shoveling while the snow is still falling down? That never made much sense to me.

MICHELE: Yep. I'd call it "Shoveling Snow." One clue is the equipment. Plastic or metal shovels. Or electric snowblowers. I asked my dad to buy us one of those, but he says why should he when he has us.

SCOTT: It is kind of fun when everyone is out shoveling after a really big snowfall.

JACOB: Especially if schools are closed.

MICHELE: It really was clever writing. The fourth graders left out some of the meaning clues like "snow" or "shovel" or "weather."

SCOTT: It's really weird. You can understand all the words, but it doesn't make sense unless you know what it's about.

JACOB: But that's like saying you have to understand it before you can understand it!

MICHELE: I guess you do have to know something about the topic before you can make predictions about what you're reading.

SCOTT: I guess that's why little kids don't understand grown-up conversations. You know the words, but not all that grown-up stuff.

JACOB: I think I understand now. Reading detectives use clues to read, but *we* have to *interpret* the clues. So we have to already know something about what we're reading in order to understand it.

DETECTIVES: *Did you figure out that Jimmy's story was about shoveling snow? Now that you know the topic, go back and read the story again. How would you change the story in order to help provide clues that would let people use their background knowledge?*

© 1999 by Debra Goodman. *From* The Reading Detective Club. *Portsmouth, NH: Heinemann.*

# DEBRIEFING:
# The Case of the Missing Titles—LaShanda's Story

! WARNING

**Read pages 133 and 135 before reading this page.**

## *Conversation*

JACOB: Well, Jimmy's article makes sense now, but LaShanda's article is completely confusing.

MICHELE: What do you mean? I don't even see what the mystery is about. I would call it "Winning at Soccer."

SCOTT: Oh, I get it now. Like she "netted" the ball—like she "scored" the winning goal.

JACOB: Well, the title doesn't help me because I don't play soccer. I've never heard of being "offsides" or a "corner kick" or a "throw in." And, to tell you the truth, I don't really care.

SCOTT: Well, I've only played a little, and we don't really have "offsides" in my league. But I understand most of it. I guess I'm a better reader than you, Jacob. Just joking!

JACOB: Hey, I bet I could write one that you wouldn't understand. I just have to think of something I know something about and you know nothing about. That shouldn't be too hard.

MICHELE: And I've been playing soccer for five years now. So it's easier to read something if you know a lot about the topic.

JACOB: Yeah, you're right. Or if you find it interesting. I'm just not that interested in understanding LaShanda's article. I mean, I'm glad she had a good game—but soccer's not my thing.

SCOTT: It's kind of like a circle.

MICHELE: What do you mean?

SCOTT: If you read about something, then you know more about it. But if you know about something, then it's easier to read about it.*

JACOB: Once in a while, you say something pretty smart, kid.

*PSST: *In other words, "You read what you are, and you are what you read."*

© 1999 by Debra Goodman.
From The Reading Detective
Club. Portsmouth, NH:
Heinemann.

*What did you think of "The Case of the Missing Titles"? Did you know that LaShanda's article was about soccer? Was it easier to read for the people in your group who play soccer? Would you like to try writing a story like Jimmy's and LaShanda's? Here are some suggestions:*

• Write about something you know how to do very well. It might be a common experience, like shoveling snow. Or it might be a special experience, like playing soccer.

• After you write your piece, go through it and take out as many meaning clues as possible. You can substitute specific words with general terms. For example, Jimmy changed *shovel* to *equipment*. He left out the word *snow* completely.

• See if your friends can guess what your piece is about.

_____

_____

_____

_____

_____

_____

_____

_____

**WHAT'S THE BIG IDEA?**

Texts have clues that help us construct meaning. But readers have to *interpret* the clues in order to understand the text. We use our experiences to interpret texts. Texts that are closer to our experiences are easier to understand. Texts that are very different from our experiences are more difficult to understand. That's why we can understand more texts as we grow older and have had more experiences. *Readers bring meaning to a text in order to make meaning with the text.*

*Want to find out more about how we read? Here comes "The Case of My Own Miscue"!*

© 1999 by Debra Goodman. *From* The Reading Detective Club. *Portsmouth, NH: Heinemann.*

# The Case of My Own Miscue

Michele was a famous detective. But today she didn't have a case. So she was reading a book. Michele loved to read.

Scott came into Michele's room. "Can I read in here with you?" he said.

"Just don't touch my things!" said Michele. Then she went back to reading.

Scott sat down on Michele's bed and began to read. After a few minutes he said, "I don't get it."

Michele didn't like to be disturbed while she was reading. "Be quiet!" she said.

"Okay," Scott said, "But I have a case for you."

Michele stopped reading to think about this. She loved to solve cases almost as much as she hated people interrupting her while she was reading.

"Oh, okay," she said. "What is it?"

"Look at this," Scott said. He showed Michele his book. It said:

> Billy parked himself in front of the teacher's desk.

"So," Michele said. "What's the mystery?"

"Well," Scott said. "Does this say he 'parked himself in front of the teacher's desk'?"

"Yeah."

"That doesn't make sense," Scott said. "When I saw *parked,* I thought Billy was driving a car, but how can he park his car in front of the teacher's desk? So that word can't be *parked.* It doesn't make sense."

Michele was getting a little confused herself. "What do you think it should say?"

Scott said, "He stood in front of the teacher's desk."

Michele said, "Okay. Does that make sense?"

Scott said, "Or maybe, 'He planted himself in front of the teacher's desk.'"

© 1999 by Debra Goodman. *From* The Reading Detective Club. *Portsmouth, NH: Heinemann.*

"That way sounds more interesting," said Michele, going back to her book. "But does he have a shovel with him in the classroom?"

DETECTIVES: *Scott could read the words in the sentence. Why was he having a problem?*

_____

_____

_____

_____

_____

_____

_____

_____

_____

_____

_____

_____

# DEBRIEFING:
# The Case of My Own Miscue

## *Conversation*

JACOB: Hey, that story was pretty funny. I used to think being a good reader meant that you get all the words right, but now I see that "making sense" is not the same as "getting the words right." Scott didn't have a problem with reading the story. He had trouble understanding why the author used the word *parked* as a metaphor for standing still.

SCOTT: A metaphor?

JACOB. Yeah. A metaphor is when you compare one thing to another. Like standing in front of a teacher's desk is like parking a car. And when you said, "He planted himself," that was another metaphor for standing still. You just liked that one better.

MICHELE: You know, we talked a lot before about "making predictions." That seemed like a really important strategy for reading detectives. But it seems like you have to do more than just make predictions to be a good reader.

JACOB: Like Scott predicted that Billy would just go stand in front of the teacher's desk.

SCOTT: When I read *parked,* I predicted that Billy was driving a car. But I knew he was in a classroom, so he couldn't be driving a car. Unless it was some kind of magical story.

MICHELE: That's what I mean. You make a prediction, but then you kind of check it out.

JACOB: If the story makes sense, you just keep reading.

SCOTT: If it doesn't make sense, you go back and fix it.

JACOB: You make a correction. It's like a correction strategy.

SCOTT: But I didn't really make it "correct." I didn't say it the way the author wrote it.

JACOB: You're right. You read it the way the author wrote it. But you didn't understand the author's words. So you used your own words to make sense out of the story.

SCOTT: Kind of like correcting the author, like we did in "The Case of the Missing Mom."

MICHELE: Well, maybe we should call them "self-checking strategies." Sometimes you notice you made a miscue that didn't make sense so you correct it, but sometimes you decide your prediction was okay. Then you probably don't even notice your miscue.

SCOTT: Or maybe you just like your prediction better.

JACOB: And sometimes you think of better words than the author's, even if you know it's a miscue.

SCOTT: I just thought I was getting Michele to help me read. But I think that was a good detective case.

JACOB: Yeah. Let's do more cases like that.

## Your Turn: The Case of My Own Miscue

DETECTIVES: *Do you want to try your own "Case of My Own Miscues"? You can try this during your regular reading time. Here's how you can get started:*

- Get something (a book, a magazine, or whatever) that you are already reading, or want to read.
- Have a few "bookmarks" ready. You can copy pages 145 and 146, and cut them into strips for bookmarks. Or make bookmarks that look like the ones on pages 145 and 146.
- Read your book.
- If you come to a section that's confusing or interesting, put your bookmark over that part.
- Keep reading until you have read for twenty or thirty minutes.
- After you've finished reading, write the entire sentence or sentences that were confusing or interesting on the "bookmark." Then answer the questions on the back.
- Take the bookmarks to your detective club meeting. Take the book, too, so you can easily get more information if you want to.
- Read your bookmark to your club members. Use the questions on the bookmark to talk about the miscue. Don't ask friends to just tell you the words. Remember, we're trying to use strategies for making your own meaning.
- You might try crossing out the section that's confusing, and try treating it like "The Case of the Missing Word." What predictions do you have for what the sentence means?
- You might brainstorm all of the possible predictions that might make sense.
- After making a number of meaning predictions, choose the one prediction that you think makes the most sense. Talk with your group about why that prediction makes the most sense.

© 1999 by Debra Goodman. *From* The Reading Detective Club. *Portsmouth, NH: Heinemann.*

## *Reading Detective Bookmark: The Case of My Own Miscue*

Name _____        Title of Book _____

The sentence(s) that I found confusing or interesting:                                    page number

_____

_____

_____

_____

_____

## *Reading Detective Bookmark: The Case of My Own Miscue*

Name _____        Title of Book _____

The sentence(s) that I found confusing or interesting:                                    page number

_____

_____

_____

_____

_____

## *Reading Detective Bookmark: The Case of My Own Miscue*

Name _____        Title of Book _____

The sentence(s) that I found confusing or interesting:                                    page number

_____

_____

_____

_____

_____

Copy these pages front and back, and then cut to make miscue bookmarks.

## *Reading Detective Bookmark: The Case of My Own Miscue, Part 2*

Name _____     Title of Book _____

The reason I found this section confusing or interesting:


Here's what I think would make sense:

---

## *Reading Detective Bookmark: The Case of My Own Miscue, Part 2*

Name _____     Title of Book _____

The reason I found this section confusing or interesting:


Here's what I think would make sense:

---

## *Reading Detective Bookmark: The Case of My Own Miscue, Part 2*

Name _____     Title of Book _____

The reason I found this section confusing or interesting:


Here's what I think would make sense:

---

Copy these pages front and back, and then cut to make miscue bookmarks.

# DEBRIEFING:
# The Reading Detective Club

## *Conversation*

JACOB: You know, readers can do some pretty amazing stuff. We can make sense out of stories with missing words. We can understand stories with mistakes in them. And we can make miscues and still make sense of what we're reading. How do we do all that?

SCOTT: We use the clues in the story to make sense out of the story.

MICHELE: We use our reading strategies, like making predictions and seeing if they turn out to be right.

JACOB: Yeah—I know all that now . . . but it just doesn't seem quite right. Isn't it important to understand the meaning of each word when we read?

MICHELE: But we all get different meanings from the same story, don't we? I think we're focusing on the big ideas . . . you know, the whole story.

SCOTT: I learn what words mean from reading a story. Words are confusing sometimes. They don't always mean the same thing. Like *can.*

JACOB: Can?

SCOTT: Like, "*Can* I use your trash *can?*"

JACOB: Oh, I get it. I guess you're right—you don't know what the words mean until you read them in a whole text.

MICHELE: Remember "The Case of the Missing Titles"? Meaning isn't in letters or words. You have to know a lot about the story ideas before you even start reading.

JACOB: I guess you're right. Meaning is in the whole thing—letter clues, word clues, language clues, and especially meaning clues. But readers have to interpret the clues to make meaning.

JACOB: Wow. I sure learned a lot about being a reading detective working with you guys. And I've changed my mind about a lot of things, too. Now I know that reading is supposed to make sense and it's okay to make mistakes.

SCOTT: I learned that we know a lot about language. Even about stuff like "nouns" that we've never heard of.

## WHAT'S THE BIG IDEA?

**Readers bring meaning to texts in order to get meaning from texts. Each reader interprets each text a little differently, because each reader has different experiences and different language understandings. We use our understandings and experiences to interpret clues and predict meanings. Each reader constructs his or her own "story." And we construct a new "story" each time we read the same text.**

MICHELE: Well, I shouldn't admit it, but I learned that certain little
brothers aren't so bad after all.

DETECTIVES: *What did you learn?*

_____

_____

_____

_____

_____

_____

_____

_____

_____

_____

_____

_____

_____

## Dear Readers,

*Congratulations. If you've finished this book, you're one smart kid! You made sense out of stories with missing words and torn pages. You even figured out stories filled with nonsense words.*

*No computer could do what you do when you read. Computers don't make mistakes because they don't construct meaning as they read. And they don't know what to do when they see a mistake. Well, they can be programmed to handle a mistake—but only people can figure out mistakes without a program to tell them what to do.*

*Only people can make meaning out of what they read. That's because the meaning isn't in the letters and the words that are printed on the page. When you read, <u>you</u> make sense out of the printed page. <u>You</u> make meaning out of what a writer has written.*

*That's why you might love to read one book, and your best friend might hate the same book. The book has a special meaning for you, but a different meaning for your friend. And you might love a book when you're six years old, but find it kind of silly when you're ten years old.*

*You also might decide that if something is too hard or too old for you to read, it's not because you can't figure out the words. It's because you haven't had the kinds of experiences you need to make sense of a writer's story. (That's why your parents like movies and books that you think are stupid, and you like movies and books that they think are stupid—at least that's how it is with my son and me.) Anyway, when you've lived a few more years, you'll probably make more sense out of those "hard" books.*

*Reading (and writing) are about making sense. It's that simple. And it's that hard. <u>You</u> are the smart kid who figured out how to do it, even before you read this book. Now you know just how smart you are! Now you're ready to go out on your own. Congratulations! You're a Certified Reading Detective (CRD).*

*Love,*

*Debi Goodman*

*P. S. In case you want to continue with your detective club, I've written up some investigations for you to try. Write me a letter and let me know how it goes. I'd love to hear from you!*

# INVESTIGATION #1:
# What Have You Read Today?

## Questions

- What do we read?
- Why do we read?

## Reason for This Investigation

What do you consider "reading"? We tend to think we are "reading" when we are reading a book for information or enjoyment. But we live in a world that is filled with print, and we read all day for many different reasons. This investigation will help you discover the many types of materials that people read, and the wide variety of reasons that people read.

## Materials

- several copies of the "What Have I Read Today?" form (on page 153)
- a pencil or pen
- a clipboard (optional)

## Collecting Clues

1. Make copies (2 or 3 per person) of the form on page 153.

2. Select a day to monitor your own reading. A weekend day is good, since you will see what you read outside of school. A weekday may be interesting as well. You might monitor two days—one weekend day and one weekday. A group of detectives might select the same day(s) so you can compare your findings.

3. Write a hypothesis about what you think you will find out. Start thinking about your own reading so you will be ready to pay attention. Share your ideas with your detective friends. What kinds of things do you think you read most? What reasons do you usually have for reading?

4. Record *everything* you read on your selected day or days, starting *from the moment you wake up in the morning.* Do you look at your clock in the morning? Do you read toothpaste tubes or cereal boxes? Try to have a normal day and don't go out of your way to read things you don't usually read. This may be hard because you're paying such close attention to your reading.

5. Fill in the column that tells what you read and how much time you spent reading (just guess—you don't need to watch the clock). You will fill in the rest of the chart later.

**The Analysis**

**1. What do we read?** After your day of recording data, look at the list of different materials that you read all day. Were you surprised at how much reading you do in a day? Fill in the "Type of Reading Material" column. For example, you might have categories, such as label, magazine, book, sign, TV ad, and so on. What types of materials do you read most often?

Now look at the time you spent reading each item. How many minutes did you spend reading each type of material? A bar graph can help you see this information clearly. Use the largest number of items or minutes to decide how many numbers you need on the left side of your graph:

| | Items Read | Minutes Reading | Items Read | Minutes Reading | Items Read | Minutes Reading |
|---|---|---|---|---|---|---|

```
5 |                        |####|                                          |####|####|    |
4 |####|####|              |####|    |####|
3 |####|####|    |    |####|####|####|    |
2 |####|####|####|####|####|####|    |####|
1 |####|####|####|####|####|####|####|####|
     labels              TV guide          advertisements
```

**2. Why do we read?** Now fill in the reasons for each of the things that you read. Some things might have more than one reason. For example, Jacob loves video games and sometimes reads *Game Pro* magazine. He reads this magazine in order to get information about the games, but he also reads it for enjoyment. How many different purposes do you have for reading? What are the most common reasons that you read?

**Discussion/Conclusions**

*What have you learned about what kinds of materials you read?* Share your findings with your fellow detectives. How are your reading choices the same or similar? How are your reading choices different?

*What are the common reasons that people read?* Can you come up with some overall categories for the type of reading that people do? For example, there's recreational (for fun), informational (to find things out), interpersonal (communicating with family and friends), occupational (for a job or required), and environmental (just because it's there).

*© 1999 by Debra Goodman. From* The Reading Detective Club. *Portsmouth, NH: Heinemann.*

You might want to make a chart or bulletin board display showing these categories with your stories or printed texts you've cut out or copied.

**Further Investigations**

• **What do people read:** Use your findings to develop a survey about what people read. Ask people who are different ages, have different jobs, and so forth. What kinds of things do all people read? What reading events are different for different people?

• **Occupational reading:** Investigate the reading and writing that adults do on the job. Interview people with different jobs. If possible, observe people at work. Do all jobs involve reading and writing? What kinds of reading and writing do workers have to do?

• **Advertisements:** Do a study of how advertisements such as billboards, newspaper ads, or TV commercials make use of print. How is print used to "sell" a product? What are the different types of advertisements? What do you think about how advertisements use print?

© 1999 by Debra Goodman.
*From* The Reading Detective
Club. *Portsmouth, NH:
Heinemann.*

## What Have I Read Today?

| Reading Event | Time Spent | Type of Material | Purpose |
|---|---|---|---|
| *example:*<br>*Crest toothpaste label* | *1 min.* | *Label* | *Make sure I brushed with*<br>*toothpaste (not Desitin)* |
| | | | |
| | | | |
| | | | |
| | | | |
| | | | |
| | | | |
| | | | |
| | | | |
| | | | |
| | | | |
| | | | |
| | | | |
| | | | |

*Make copies of this chart if you need more pages.*

# INVESTIGATION #2:
# Easy as Falling off a Bicycle

## Question

- How do we learn?

## Reason for This Investigation

Learning to read and write is a lot like learning other things. But it's hard to talk about how we *learned* to read and write because most of us learned to read and write in school. When we think about learning to read, we might get mixed up between how we *learned* to read and how we *were taught* to read. If a teacher started by teaching us the alphabet, we think that's how we learned to read. If a teacher started by reading us Big Books and having us read along, we think that's how we learned to read. You probably didn't learn how to ride a bicycle in school. So we're not as likely to confuse learning and teaching. Talking about how we learned to ride a bicycle helps us to focus on how learning happens.

NOTE: *If you or your friends don't ride bicycles, you can pick a different learning experience to investigate. Pick something you learned to do just for fun, such as learning to swim, rollerblade, dance, play basketball. The only rule is that you must have learned how to do the activity without taking a class.*

## Group

This investigation will work well with a small group of detectives. It can also be a whole-class investigation.

## Materials

- paper and pencil to write or draw
- a tape recorder and tapes (optional)

## Collecting Clues

1. Think about how you learned to ride a bicycle. (Remember, if you don't ride a bicycle, choose something else you enjoy doing, such as ice skating or shooting baskets.) You may want to talk with your family, since they might remember things that you don't remember.

2. Make an outline (list) of some of the things you remember. You can write your story down or draw pictures of your bike-riding adventures.

© 1999 by Debra Goodman.
From The Reading Detective Club. Portsmouth, NH: Heinemann.

3. Ask friends to tell you how they learned to ride a bicycle. Jot down some of the details from their stories. You might tape-record the stories so you can listen to them again later. Or you can publish them in a class book.

## The Analysis

1. Share the stories you collected with your group. Listen to their stories as well.

2. Write each of the events of your story on a sticky note or note card.

3. Get together with your group and organize your note cards into big categories. Can you come up with four or five general categories of "How we learn"?

*© 1999 by Debra Goodman.*
*From* The Reading Detective
Club. *Portsmouth, NH:*
*Heinemann.*

**How we learn:**

We wanted to learn
I saw the big kids riding and wanted to ride.

I got a new bike for my birthday.

Grown-ups helped us
My mom held onto my bike seat and ran along behind me.

My first bike had training wheels. My dad kept putting them higher and higher.

We practiced and practiced
I rode my bike every single day.

I kept trying and trying until I could ride no handed.

We fell down a lot
At first I didn't know how to stop and so I crashed into a tree!

When I was trying to pop a wheelie I kept falling off the back of the bike

4. Make a name for your categories of story events (such as "falling down"). Write these titles down and choose two or three interesting comments from different stories to use for examples of your category. You now have a report that you can share with other detectives.

**Discussion/Conclusions**

After you have finished your investigation, you might consider the following questions:

1. What does this investigation tell you about how and WHY we learn?
2. Is learning how to ride a bike similar to learning how to read?

© 1999 by Debra Goodman. From The Reading Detective Club. Portsmouth, NH: Heinemann.

One way to compare bike riding to learning to read is to look at each category and think about reading and writing. In classes that I've worked with, we often end up with these basic categories:

WE LEARN WHEN

1. **We want to.** Few children are ever forced to ride a bike. Do we also learn to read because we want to? Is it easier to learn to read if we want to read? What makes children want to read?

2. **We practice.** But we practice riding bikes by riding. It doesn't help to learn how to steer first, and then how to work the pedals. Do we also practice reading by reading real books, magazines, and so forth? Will reading more and more make us better readers?

3. **We fall down.** Learning always involves making mistakes. Good baseball players have a .300 batting average. That means they hit the ball only 3 out of 10 times at bat. And we never stop falling down. That's why even expert bike riders wear helmets. If we're going faster or trying a new stunt, we're likely to fall. Are mistakes an important part of learning to read? Can you learn to read without making mistakes?

4. **We get help.** But the help is just what we need and when we need it. Sometimes just watching other people ride is all the help we need. Sometimes we want someone to hold us up until we can balance the bike ourselves. What kind of help do readers need? What is the best way to help a beginning reader?

5. **We have a bicycle.** Some of us live in places where there are no bicycles. Or maybe our parents don't have the money to buy us a bicycle. Can you learn to read without books, paper, or pencils? How many books do you need? Where should the books be so everyone can read them? When should you be able to read them?

**Further Investigations**

• **A reading autobiography:** Now that you've thought about learning outside of school, you might want to think about some early learning-to-read experiences. Remember you had reading experiences outside of school and inside school. Categorize these stories like you did with the bicycle riding. What do you remember about learning to read? Did these experiences help you to learn to read? Was learning to read easy or difficult? Why?

• **Observing young children learning to read:** Ask a kindergarten or a first-grade teacher if you can come into the classroom while the children are reading. Make a list of the things you see while you are in the classroom. Try to observe one or two children to see what they are doing during the reading time. After watching a few times, you might want to make a list of questions to ask the teacher and some of the students. What do you notice about young children who are learning to read?

- **Helping young children with reading:** If we learn to read by practicing (reading and writing), how can we help young children with reading? One way is to read to them. But busy teachers don't always have time to read to every child in the classroom. Your detective club might volunteer to be "book buddies" with young children. You can read them stories and you can listen to them when they start reading.

© 1999 by Debra Goodman.
From The Reading Detective
Club. Portsmouth, NH:
Heinemann.

# INVESTIGATION #3:
# Studying Our Own Miscues

## Questions

- What miscues do you make when you read?
- How do your miscues show what you know about language?
- What smart reading strategies do you use when you read?

## Reason for This Investigation

This investigation allows you to explore your own reading in depth. It helps you see that reading is a process of making meaning. When you study your own miscues, you realize that miscues show smart thinking. They are not careless or lazy reading. As you study your own miscues, you will find out what strategies and clues you usually use when you read. The investigation helps you to know your own strengths as a reader.

NOTE TO READERS AND ADULT HELPERS: *Miscues show how smart you are. Don't worry if you have a lot of miscues when you read. Make sure you look carefully for all of the good thinking you were doing. And give yourself a pat on the back for searching for meaning in text.*

## Groups

You will need a partner. You will take turns being the reader and the listener. You might ask an adult to help you at first.

## Materials

- a text (book, magazine, or the like) that you are reading. It should be a little challenging for you to read, and something you haven't read before
- a tape recorder and blank tape
- copies of the pages you are reading to the tape recorder (optional)
- pencils
- the "Reader's Own Miscue" form (see page 164)

## Collecting Clues

1. Testing the recorder: Place a blank tape in the tape recorder. Say your names, the title of the text, and the current date. Check to make sure the tape recorder is working before you record the reading.

© 1999 by Debra Goodman. From The Reading Detective Club. Portsmouth, NH: Heinemann.

2. The reading:

- **Reader:** Read your book, magazine article, or chapter (or one chapter if it is a long book) into the tape recorder. Use your own strategies if you have any problems, and don't ask the listeners for help. For example, if you come to something you're not sure of, use any strategy you usually use. Remember that it's okay to guess (or predict).
- **Listener:** Have a copy of the section that the reader is reading. Read along silently as the reader reads the text. If the reader says something different from your own reading, make a note or underline that section.

3. The retelling: After the reader is finished, the reader should put the text aside and retell everything she or he can remember from the text. When the reader is done retelling, the listener might retell what he or she remembers.

4. Second reader: After the first reading is completed, switch jobs so that both partners have a chance to read. Repeat parts 1 to 3 with a new listener and reader.

5. Listening to the tape: Have copies of the text in front of you and listen to the taped story. If either the reader or listener hears a miscue, yell "stop." Stop the tape, rewind it a little, and listen again. Underline or mark your copies where the reader says something you were not expecting. (If you are not using copies, you can mark the miscues with sticky notes.) Keep listening and taking notes until you have heard the entire tape.

- If you have a long text, you might not listen to the entire tape. Skip a few pages and start after the reader is "warmed up." Stop recording miscues after you have twenty recorded (or get to the end of the text).

6. Selecting miscues to study: Skip the first few pages of reading, since the reader is just getting "warmed up." Select the next five or six sentences that include miscues. Skip any miscues that are exactly the same. (You can also choose five miscues that seem interesting.)

7. Recording the miscues: Now use your Reader's Own Miscue form to record your miscues. Write down the whole sentence the way the reader read it after all corrections, and how it is printed in the book. Listen to the tape recorder one more time as you do the writing. The reader and listener should agree on the "reader's reading" and the "written text."

© 1999 by Debra Goodman. *From* The Reading Detective Club. *Portsmouth, NH: Heinemann.*

## *Recording the Miscues: An Example*

Printed Text: *In my building everyone owns a dog.*

Reader says: *On my block . . . building . . . In my building every - . . . everyone is . . . has a dog.*

In this example, the reader has many substitutions. She reads *on* for *in, block* for *building,* and *is* for *owns.* However, most of the miscues are corrected. The miscue *is* for *owns* is changed to *has.* The reader's final reading is how the reader reads the sentence AFTER all changes or corrections:

| Page number: | **Reader's final reading** (write the entire sentence) In my building everyone has a dog. |
| --- | --- |
| 1 | **The printed text** (write the entire sentence) In my building everyone owns a dog. |

### The Analysis

After you have filled in the sentences on the Reader's Own Miscue form, you will use the miscue questions to begin analyzing your reading strategies.

**1. Why Did the Reader Make the Miscue? What Strategies Was the Reader Using?** All miscues are made because you are using language strategies. So don't say, "I was careless" or "I wasn't thinking." In fact, you were thinking. The reader and listener should try to decide what you were thinking when you made each miscue. *What strategies was the reader using?* As the reader were you so busy predicting story meaning that you used your own language instead of the text? Did the miscue make sense with what came before it?

**2. What Clues Was the Reader Using?** If the sentence makes sense, then the reader is predicting and correcting using the *meaning clues.* If the sentence doesn't make sense, then the reader might have been focusing on other clues. Was the reader using language clues? If the reader was using language clues then the sentence will "sound like English." Was the reader using graphic clues? If the reader was using graphic clues, then the substitution will look similar to the printed text. Remember, the reader may have been using more than one type of clue at the same time.

**3. Did the Reader Correct the Miscues? Do You Think They Should Have Been Corrected?** If the miscue does not affect the meaning of the story, then a miscue probably doesn't have to be

© *1999 by Debra Goodman. From* The Reading Detective Club. *Portsmouth, NH: Heinemann.*

corrected. If the miscue interferes with the reader's ability to understand the story, is there a better guess or prediction the reader could have made?

**4. Does the Miscue Change the Meaning of the Text?** This is a tricky question because you need to think about the entire text. Was the reader able to understand this text with this miscue? Remember, some words in sentences are not as important as others. If the miscue (before it was corrected) would make it difficult to understand the text, write "yes." If the miscue may cause some problems with making meaning, write "some." If the miscue didn't really change the meaning of the whole text, write "no."

### Use the "Reader's Own Miscue Profile" (page 165) to Think About Your Reading

Listen to the retelling and think about how you were able to *make sense* of the story. Use the profile sheet on page 165 to think about your strategies. First focus on the good reading strategies you used. Then think about some strategies you might try next time.

### Discussion/Conclusions

Get together with other detectives and share your findings. Talk about how miscues show us our thinking process while we read. Talk about all of the smart things you did when you were reading. Talk about which strategies and clues helped you understand the text.

You might make some charts that reflect your discussion. For example: What is a "good miscue"? Good miscues help us get meaning from the text. What kinds of miscues help us? Make a list of the "good miscues" in your own readings.

### Further Investigations

• **Continue the miscue study:** If you enjoyed looking at these miscues, you might want to repeat the procedure and look at more miscues. You can also use this procedure several times during the year and see how your reading strategies change and improve.

• **Investigating miscues:** Pick out one kind of miscue and make a study of that type of miscue. Go back to the tapes and recorded miscues and write down examples of that type. Why do these miscues occur? What is the reader thinking? What strategies and clues are involved? How are these miscues helpful or not helpful in understanding the text?

Here are some examples of studying one type of miscue:
• **Omissions:** skipping a part of the text. Sometimes readers "skip" a word or phrase, but sometimes they aren't aware that they have "skipped" a part of the text. When and why do these types of omissions occur?

• **Meaningful substitutions:** substituting language that has the same meaning as the language in the text. Was the reader aware of the substitution? Why do these miscues occur? What strategies are involved? How do they affect story meaning?

• **Repeated miscues:** having many miscues on the same word or phrase. What does the reader do when unfamiliar text is used many times? Does the reader stick to one prediction or one reading strategy? Is the reader able to eventually "figure out" the text? Does the reader understand what the unfamiliar text means? (Use retellings and talk to readers.) How does the text provide clues that help the reader understand the meaning of the word or phrase?

• **Language variations and dialect:** Sometimes the reader and author, or reader and listener, have different ways of speaking and writing. It's important to know that everyone speaks a dialect or variation of English. No variation is better than another. There are two types of miscues involving variations:

1. The author uses a language unfamiliar to the reader. A group of readers were confused by *polecat* in a book that takes place in the south. The text didn't provide much information, especially since the word was used for name calling: "you low down polecat." In other cases, authors use "eye dialect"—writing how a person talks instead of using conventional spellings. For example, "'I'm gon' get him yet,' she say, turning 'round and 'round." Did this happen in any of your texts? How do readers respond to unfamiliar language variations in texts?

2. Where the reader and listener use different variations. One reader read *s'pozd* for the text *supposed*. This is not really a miscue, because she is saying the word *supposed* in her own language. Some listeners pronounce the word differently: *sa-pozd*. (Notice that neither reader says *supposed* the way the text is written.) Did you have examples where readers and listeners pronounce words differently? Do these differences interfere with understanding the text?

## Reader's Own Miscue Form

**Reader's Name:** _____ **Title of Book:** _____

**Page
number:**

    **The reader's response** (write the entire sentence)

_____

    **The printed text** (write the entire sentence)

_____     _____

**1. Strategies:** What was the reader thinking? What strategies did the reader use?

_____

_____

_____

**2. Clues:** What clues was the reader using?

_____

_____

_____

**3. Correction:** Did the reader correct the miscue? Do you think it should have been corrected?

_____

_____

_____

**4. Meaning change:** Did the miscue change the meaning of the text? Why or why not?

_____

_____

_____

## Reader's Own Miscue Profile

**Reader's Name:** _____ **Title of Book:** _____

Did the miscues change the meaning of the text?

_____

_____

If the miscues did change the text meaning, were they corrected?

_____

_____

What strategies helped you make sense of the story?

_____

_____

What strategies will you try the next time you read?

_____

_____

What have you learned about reading?

_____

_____

What have you learned about yourself?

_____

_____

# INVESTIGATION #4:
# Journal Buddies—
# Exploring Invented Spellings

## Questions

- How do young children learn to write?
- What do invented spellings show us about children's learning?

## Reason for This Investigation

If you have younger brothers and sisters, you have probably seen them scribble and write strings of letters across a page. But did you know that this is how your sister and brother are learning how to write? This investigation will help you understand how young children learn to write by inventing the rules for how to write and spell.

## Materials

- a notebook or journal
- pencils and drawing materials
- a group of young children (ages five through seven will work out well)

## Collecting Clues

1. Volunteer to be journal buddies—or pen pals—with a group of younger children (kindergarten through second grade). Each member of your detective club can work with one younger child.

2. Select a journal or notebook and write a short letter to your journal buddy. Tell about yourself and ask your young buddy some questions. You might draw a picture to go with your letter.

3. If possible, meet with your buddy and read them your letter. Then ask them to write a letter back to you on the next page. Encourage the younger child to write and spell the best they can. Try not to spell words for them (or you won't have anything to investigate). If they say they can't write or spell, try telling them to just "pretend" to write or spell. Tell them you want to know how young kids learn to write without older kids helping.

4. After the young child is finished writing, ask them to read what they wrote to you. You might write their story down in smaller print at the bottom of the page so that you can remember it later.

5. If you can't meet with your buddy, ask the teacher (or parent) to have your buddy write you a letter back. Tell the teacher that you are looking at invented spellings, and you don't mind if the letter is not "perfect."

6. Keep writing back and forth with your journal buddy as often as you can. This will help you to see how young children's writing changes and grows over time.

## The Analysis of Young Children's Writing

**How Do Young Children Learn to Write?** Before looking at the invented spellings, take a look at what your buddy is writing. Are they writing a message expressing their own thoughts or ideas? Are they writing stories or letters? Are their letters getting longer over time? Are they using interesting words and ideas?

## How Does Invented Spelling Show Us That Children Are Learning?

- First look for words that your buddy knows how to spell. How many words did they spell the "grown-up" way?

- If your buddy scribbles or writes strings of letters, are they written in a row like "real" writing? Do they include some of the words from your letters, like *dear* or *love*? How do they change over time?

- If your child used invented spellings, what strategies did your buddy use to develop the spelling?
  Are they using the beginning letters?
    I like my friend. = I L M F
  Are they using the consonant sounds?
    I like my friend = I LK M FD
  Are they writing words the way they sound?
    I LIK MI FRED
  Are they using numbers or letters to represent words?
    U R GD 2 ME
  Are they starting to generalize about spelling rules? For
    example, using $y$ to spell $e$ sounds?

- You can also make a list of invented spellings and compare them to the "grown-up" spelling. How close are they? You might make a record of the invented spellings of the same words whenever they come up:

```
LIKE
9/1      L
10/5     LK
10/20    LIK
11/15    LIKE
12/1     LIEK
12/15    LIKE
```

## Discussion/Conclusions

Get together with other detectives and compare your children's writing:
- What do you notice about how their letters change over time? Do they write more? Do they use interesting words?
- Do you notice your buddy using your letter as a model? Do they answer your questions? Do they begin to pick up some of your language and spelling patterns?
- What do you notice about young children's spellings? Are your buddy's invented spellings similar to other detective club members'? Do you see any patterns?
- What do you notice about your buddy's writing and spelling over time? Do they use more "grown-up" spellings? Do their spellings look more and more similar to "grown-up" spellings?

When young children write with invented spellings, they are inventing the spelling rules of our language. Our spelling rules are very complicated. How do you observe young children learning the rules and patterns for English spellings?

## Further Investigations

• **Spelling patterns:** You might start a class study of spelling patterns. Choose certain patterns that you notice. You might select words that use the same pattern, such as *date, fate, mate,* and so on. Then you might look for words that you predict might have the same pattern, but they don't, such as *bait, great, eight,* and so forth.

• **Spelling problems:** You can do a survey asking children and adults what words they always have problems spelling. Make a list of these words. See if you can figure out what the p1roblem is. Can you figure out a rules that will explain how to spell the words? If you do, try to find exceptions to the rule just to make sure it works.

© 1999 by Debra Goodman.
*From* The Reading Detective
Club. *Portsmouth, NH:
Heinemann.*